PENGUIN CLASSICS

GORGIAS

PLATO (*c.* 427–347 BC) stands with Socrates and Aristotle as one of the shapers of the whole intellectual tradition of the West. He came from a family that had long played a prominent part in Athenian politics, and it would have been natural for him to follow the same course. He declined to do so, however, disillusioned by the violence and corruption of Athenian political life, and especially by the execution in 399 of his friend and teacher, Socrates. Inspired by Socrates' enquiries into the nature of ethical standards, Plato sought a cure for the ills of society, not in politics but in philosophy, and arrived at his fundamental and lasting conviction that those ills would never cease until philosophers became rulers or rulers philosophers. At an uncertain date in the early fourth century BC he founded in Athens the Academy, the first permanent institution devoted to philosophical research and teaching, and the prototype of all Western universities. On several occasions he travelled to Sicily in an attempt to put his political theories into practice, notably as an adviser to Dionysius II, ruler of Syracuse.

Plato wrote over twenty philosophical dialogues, and there are also extant under his name thirteen letters, whose genuineness is keenly disputed. His literary activity extended over half a century; few other writers have exploited so effectively the grace and precision, the flexibility and power, of Greek prose.

WALTER HAMILTON was master of Magdalene College, Cambridge, from 1967 to 1978, and then was made an Honorary Fellow. Born in 1908, he was a Scholar of Trinity College Cambridge, where he gained first class honours in both parts of the Classical Tripos. He was a Fellow of Trinity College and a University Lecturer at Cambridge, and taught at Eton before becoming Headmaster of Westminster School (1950–57) and of Rugby School (1957–66). He translated Ammianus Marcellinus' *The Later Roman Empire* and Plato's *Symposium* and his *Phaedrus and Letters VII and VIII* all for Penguin Classics. Walter Hamilton died in 1988.

CHRIS EMLYN-JONES studied at Birmingham University, where he received his PhD in 1972. Since 1979, he has taught in the department of Classical Studies at the Open University. His publications include *The Ionians and Hellenism* (1980), *Homer: Readings and Images* (co-editor) (1992), commentaries on the Greek texts of a number of Plato's early dialogues, and various articles on Plato, the Presocratics and Homer. His hobby is music-making, instrumental and vocal.

PLATO
Gorgias

REVISED EDITION

Translated by
WALTER HAMILTON *and* CHRIS EMLYN-JONES
Introduction, Commentary and Notes by
CHRIS EMLYN-JONES

PENGUIN BOOKS

PENGUIN BOOKS

Published by the Penguin Group
Penguin Books Ltd, 80 Strand, London WC2R 0RL, England
Penguin Putnam Inc., 375 Hudson Street, New York, New York 10014, USA
Penguin Books Australia Ltd, 250 Camberwell Road, Camberwell, Victoria 3124, Australia
Penguin Books Canada Ltd, 10 Alcorn Avenue, Toronto, Ontario, Canada M4V 3B2
Penguin Books India (P) Ltd, 11 Community Centre, Panchsheel Park, New Delhi – 110 017, India
Penguin Books (NZ) Ltd, Cnr Rosedale and Airborne Roads, Albany, Auckland, New Zealand
Penguin Books (South Africa) (Pty) Ltd, 24 Sturdee Avenue, Rosebank 2196, South Africa

Penguin Books Ltd, Registered Offices: 80 Strand, London WC2R 0RL, England

www.penguin.com

First published 1960
Revised edition 2004
9

Set in 10.25/12.25 pt PostScript Adobe Sabon
Typeset by Rowland Phototypesetting Ltd, Bury St Edmunds, Suffolk
Printed in England by Clays Ltd, St Ives plc

ISBN-13: 978–0–140–44904–4

Contents

Gorgias

Acknowledgements

I would like to thank Rosemary Wright for helpful comment on an early draft of the Introduction, Translation and Commentary; I am also grateful to Louise Mansfield and Lynda White for technical assistance in the preparation of the manuscript.

Chris Emlyn-Jones
January 2003

Reference System Used in this Edition

Bibliographical references

References to modern scholarly works in the Introduction and Commentary are to author and date of publication and, where appropriate, page numbers, e.g. 'Dodds 1959, p. 250'. This relates to the Further Reading, where full details of the publication can be found.

References to the translation and commentary

The running section numbers and sub-section letters in the margin of the translation (e.g. 467b . . . c etc.) approximate to the pages and smaller divisions of the Greek text of the sixteenth-century AD edition of Stephanus, which is standard in all modern editions (and most translations) of Plato; quite apart from allowing precision of reference, this system will aid the reader wishing to use this translation alongside a Greek text.

The sectional divisions of *Gorgias*, (A[1], B[3], etc.) are purely editorial and are placed at what I judge to be suitable breaks in the dialogue, although there is rarely an obvious dramatic break, since Plato's usual method of composition was to disguise, rather than signal, changes of subject.

The letters A, B and C correspond to the main tripartite structure of the dialogue, the successive conversations with Gorgias, Polus and Callicles. The smaller divisions [1], [2] etc. represent coherent sections suitable for editorial explanation and comment. The method adopted is to preface a section with an introductory explanation, leaving until the end of the section, where appropriate, discussion on points of interest and/or difficulty. Notes are restricted to the elucidation of more specific detail.

Chronology

Many of the events and the chronology of Plato's life as well as the dates and order of the composition of his dialogues cannot be established with any certainty and are still a matter of lively debate; the following represents a general, but not universal, consensus. Works of disputed authorship have not been included. All dates are BC.

c. 427 Birth of Plato from an old and wealthy Athenian family.

404 Defeat of Athens in the war with Sparta (the Peloponnesian War).

403 The rule of a right-wing junta in Athens (the 'Thirty Tyrants'), involving his relatives, followed by the restoration of democracy.

399 The trial, condemnation and execution of Socrates on a charge of 'not acknowledging the gods which the city acknowledges, but introducing new divinities and corrupting the youth'.

390s–early 80s Following the death of Socrates, Plato and other followers of Socrates withdraw from Athens to the nearby city of Megara. Plato travels extensively.

Composition of the short Early period dialogues: *Apology*, *Crito*, *Charmides*, *Euthyphro*, *Hippias Minor*, *Ion*, *Laches*, *Lysis*.

389/8 Visits Italy and Sicily, probably in order to make contact with Pythagorean philosophers.

c. 387 Founds the Academy on the site of the shrine of the hero Academus in the north-west district of Athens.

380s The later Early period dialogues: *Gorgias*, *Menexenus*, *Protagoras*.

late 380s The Middle period dialogues: *Cratylus*, *Euthydemus*, *Meno*, *Phaedo*.

370s The later Middle period dialogues: *Parmenides*, *Phaedrus*, *Symposium*, *Republic*, *Theaetetus*.

367 Visits Sicily for a second time at the invitation of Dion, uncle of the young Dionysius II, ruler of Syracuse, in the hope of influencing the government of the city. The attempt was unsuccessful. Aristotle joins the Academy.

360s–50s The Late period dialogues: *Critias*, *Philebus*, *Sophist*, *Statesman*, *Timaeus*.

361 Final visit to Sicily, ending again in failure to influence Dionysius.

late 350s Final dialogue: *Laws*.

347 Death of Plato.

Introduction

The cultural background

Plato's dialogue *Gorgias*, though firmly set in the cultural world of the late fifth and early fourth centuries BC, debates questions which perennially face people who give thought as to how they should govern or be governed, and what should be the qualifications required of those who aspire to public office. Are high moral standards essential, or should we give our preference to the pragmatist who gets things done, or negotiates successfully? Is the power of rulers to do as they wish a force to be admired, especially if they affect the lives of countless others? Behind these questions lie other more basic issues concerning how we all ought to live our lives: ought we to aim to maximize our pleasure and that of others or should our overriding concern be to act virtuously? And how can our choice be justified?

We might be moved at this point to object that choices in real life are rarely that simple; between such stark alternatives there is much middle ground. Yet the posing of these questions in a sharply polarized form – either virtue or pleasure – reflects the presentation of confrontations between the philosopher Socrates and a variety of representatives of contemporary Athenian society, powerfully dramatized in Plato's dialogues, and never more so than in *Gorgias*. The four participants in this debate lay claim to the most potent of the positive values in the Athenian ethical armoury: excellence and happiness; but what they each mean by these words is very different, and what emerges is a contest between two opposed ways of life – one occupied with the maximization of pleasure through the exercise of worldly power and the other concerned with moral absolutes such as justice and goodness.

Two of Socrates' three interlocutors, Gorgias and Polus, are orators, experts in the public speaking of the day, and it is this topic which opens the dialogue:[1] Socrates wants to find out exactly what is the nature of Gorgias' expertise in this area. Soon, however, they move from this to the subject of political power – not an entirely obvious transition, you might think. However, the small agriculturally based self-governing political unit characteristic of the Classical Greek world, the city (*polis*), was very much a 'face-to-face' society, in which the ability to speak persuasively in front of large audiences was an essential qualification for a successful political career, especially, it appears, in Athens, where major political decisions, including such vital matters as declarations of war, were taken by an Assembly in which all citizens were entitled to speak and vote. Even in Athens citizens were still a minority of the population; there were slaves and resident foreigners, and women took no part in public life. Nevertheless, the Athenians were proud of having a society which was at least more politically inclusive than others. In such an environment oratorical skill really could mean power and influence, and was clearly a significant factor in the domination of the democratic Assembly by such statesmen as Pericles (*c.* 495–429). The same skill could be applied in the Athenian law courts, where to be clever at speaking was a definite advantage for those performing in front of juries of several hundred of their fellow citizens.

Early in Plato's dialogue, Gorgias boasts that his art, that of the skilled orator, gives an individual 'the greatest good, which confers on everyone who possesses it not only freedom for himself but also the power of ruling his fellow-citizens' (452d5). The power of speech to control people's thoughts and emotions was celebrated by the historical Gorgias in an oration which sought to defend the notorious Helen of Troy; she was helpless in the face of the blandishments of her lover Paris: 'Speech is a mighty ruler which with the minutest and most invisible body accomplishes the most godlike deeds'.[2]

Whether or not the power of eloquent speech was indeed 'the

greatest good', as Plato's Gorgias claims, the Athenians of the fifth century BC distinguished themselves from their neighbours and enemies as a society whose citizens thoroughly debated important issues before taking action.[3] The need for aspiring Athenian politicians to acquire this vital adjunct to political success was met by a group of professionals to which Gorgias belonged; they were known collectively as sophists – itinerant teachers of the skills of persuasive speaking, for whom Athens was the most important centre in Greece.[4] These teachers supplied, for a fee, a kind of higher education for those who could afford it, which included the introduction of topics on which their pupils might exercise their acquired eloquence; these typically focused on social issues, such as, for example, whether life in communities like the *polis* and other societies had developed by nature (*physis*) or through the application of conventional human laws and customs (the product of 'law' = *nomos*). The practical implications of such issues became clear when they emerged from the classroom and into the public arena in a tragedy like Sophocles' *Antigone* (*c*. 442 BC), where a crowded theatre witnessed hot debate between the Theban ruler Creon and the princess Antigone over whether her actions in granting her brother burial rites were bound by the laws and decrees of the state or whether she answered to the unwritten ('natural') edicts of the gods.[5] Self-conscious analysis and criticism of traditional myths and stories also went hand-in-hand with speculation about the more obvious aspects of *physis* – the nature of the gods and the origin of the universe. At the end of Sophocles' play, the 'laws of the gods' reassert their power over a broken Creon; but there is evidence of a more thoroughgoing scepticism, for example in a fragment from a play (*Sisyphus*) of disputed authorship,[6] where it is suggested that the idea of deity was invented by humans to prevent injustice, and that the gods are as much a part of convention (*nomos*) as the society they allegedly created.

The question that concerned Plato was whether Gorgias, and the orators and sophists in general, also taught their students to consider the moral consequences of their activity (see *Gorgias*, A[6]). This concern was already in the public consciousness in the later fifth century, as, for example, the comic dramatist Aristophanes shows in his play *Clouds*, the skill of speaking effectively was also seen as the ability to 'make the weaker argument the stronger',[7] and to turn conventional morality upside down for personal advantage. Aristophanes' principal character, a rascally old farmer, Strepsiades, simply wants to find a way of getting out of paying the debts incurred by his horse-mad son. But such debates could take on much more serious and wide-ranging implications: the relationship of moral values to state and inter-state politics is one of the key themes of the historian Thucydides, who charted the course of the major conflict between Athens and Sparta which stretched through the last quarter of the fifth century. In Thucydides' *History of the Peloponnesian War* politicians are given speeches in which lip-service to values such as justice and temperance masks a belief in the all-governing desire for power: as the Athenians say to the unfortunate inhabitants of the mid-Aegean island of Melos, who contemplate resistance to Athenian forces (416 BC): 'Our opinion of the gods and our knowledge of men lead us to conclude that it is a general and necessary law of nature to rule whatever one can.'[8] Thucydides' speeches were not verbatim reports, any more than Aristophanes' or Sophocles' plays were real life; but these diverse sources suggest that debates about values were within the consciousness of the man-in-the-street as well as the preoccupation of intellectuals.

Socrates and Plato

The man to whom Strepsiades goes to find a way out of his troubles in Aristophanes' play (see above) is Socrates, the alternately pompous and sly head of a school of subversive intellectual investigation, humorously dubbed a 'thinking-shop'. Other comic dramatists featured Socrates, whose distinctive appearance, to judge from later busts and contemporary verbal portraits, had considerable humorous potential; he is portrayed as short and squat, with snub nose and bulging eyes. The historical character (*c.* 469–399), what sort of man he was and what he did, is harder to capture; unlike the sophists, he wrote nothing, and we rely on a number of accounts, of which the most important, besides the comedy-writers, are those of Xenophon (428–*c*. 354) and Plato (*c*. 427–347), both of them followers and associates. These two portraits of Socrates coincide to the limited extent that both picture a man concerned with discussing morality, and certainly not engaged in the speculative scientific activity parodied by Aristophanes or the teaching of persuasive speech, like Gorgias. Beyond this they tend to diverge; Xenophon's character is a rather conventional moralist, while Plato's Socrates is the intellectually acute and ironic questioner who gathered groups of young men around him in public places in Athens, such as gymnasia – where younger Athenians, mainly upper-class, took physical exercise and relaxed – and the market-place (Agora), continually asking the sort of questions which open the dialogue *Gorgias*: what professional individuals profess, and how what they do relates to key moral values such as justice, piety, temperance and excellence in general.[9]

Plato's Socrates claims to differ from the sophists in two major respects: he does not charge fees and (or because) he does not impart knowledge with a view to promoting his pupils' success; indeed, he does not claim to know anything for certain but elicits knowledge from his associates by means of asking them questions. The degree to which Socrates' professions of ignorance are ironically conceived is debatable; as we shall shortly see from *Gorgias*, Plato's Socrates does on occasion make quite substantial claims to knowledge. His Athenian contemporaries certainly thought that he did; in 399 BC, in one of the few pieces of evidence for the historical Socrates which is firmly established, he was prosecuted for impiety, condemned and executed by means of the drinking of hemlock. The indictment on which he was found guilty – 'not acknowledging the gods which the city acknowledges, but introducing new divinities, and corrupting the youth' – may have been a trumped-up charge to cover suspicion of other more political associations.

The Spartan victory in 404 BC at the end of the long drawn-out Peloponnesian War led to right-wing revolution in Athens and the establishment of a junta known as the 'Thirty Tyrants', under whose rule a reign of terror was instituted. Following the fall of this short-lived government, democratic rule was re-established, with a political amnesty. In the famous defence speech which Plato gives to him, the *Apology*, Socrates seeks to distance himself from partisan politics in order to portray himself as an unpopular but politically detached critic of contemporary Athenian society, the stinging gadfly which stimulates the large thoroughbred horse by questioning the Athenians' basic moral values.[10] However, it is possible, and later generations certainly believed, that Socrates was charged and condemned at least partly by reason of his association with a number of people prominent in the earlier junta, such as the sophist Critias, and earlier on, élitist politicians such as Alcibiades, an accusation which the political amnesty may have ruled out of court.[11]

Plato came from a well-to-do family which associated with Pericles and was related to right-wing figures, his cousins Critias and Charmides. During Socrates' lifetime Plato appears to have been just one of a number of his younger associates, and we know nothing about his personal relationship with Socrates either from contemporary sources or from later accounts.[12] After Socrates' death, however, a number of former followers composed commemorative memoirs which presented versions of Socrates' life and beliefs through works which purported to recall their master's informal style of teaching, the so-called Socratic conversations. With the exception of Plato and Xenophon, these survive only in fragmentary form.[13] Plato's dialogues are formally part of this genre, but in scope and literary quality go far beyond it. The commemorative element in his Socrates, although almost never entirely absent, was transformed into a philosophical exploration of great originality which, while doubtless taking its origin from the conversations of the historical Socrates and continuing to use his name, developed ideas far beyond anything that Socrates conceived.

The effect of Socrates' death on Plato can perhaps be gauged from a letter, the seventh from a collection of thirteen, allegedly written by him later in his life to friends and associates of his Sicilian friend Dion, a devoted Platonist and a relation of Dionysius I and II, successive rulers of Syracuse. The authenticity of the letters has long been disputed, but the Seventh, if not by

Plato, may well have been written during his lifetime, and may give some idea of his reaction to the events described above. The charge against Socrates he regarded as 'most sacrilegious, which he least of all people deserved'. The government which followed was, he considered, irredeemably corrupt, and the natural progression for someone of his class, to go into active politics, was one he felt unable to take. '[The result was] that I, who began full of enthusiasm for a political career, ended by growing dizzy at the spectacle of universal confusion . . . but finally I came to the conclusion that the condition of all existing states is bad . . . and that the troubles of mankind will never cease until either true and genuine philosophers attain political power or the rulers of states by some dispensation of providence become genuine philosophers.'[14]

This may well be putting a retrospective gloss on what were in fact only gradual stages in Plato's development. Moreover the sentiments of the Seventh Letter bear a suspicious resemblance to attitudes towards Athenian political life which Plato's Socrates expresses in, for example, *Gorgias* and *Republic*; therefore we cannot be entirely safe in making inferences from the Letter to the dialogues rather than vice versa. Nevertheless, it is certain that after Socrates' death Plato did not go into politics, but, after a period of withdrawal from Athens, returned and at some stage in the 390s–80s founded a school on the site of the shrine of the hero Academus, in the north-west quarter of the city of Athens.

For Plato, seclusion did not mean ivory-tower isolation; the concern for good government and Utopian ideals which comes through in the Letter remained a preoccupation of his, and he established close relations with intellectuals in Sicily and in particular Dion (see above). He made three journeys to Sicily in the course of his life, the second in 367 at the request of Dion, in a desire to influence the young Dionysius II, who had become ruler on his father's death, to take up his Utopian vision. These attempts, supposedly to influence the creation of a 'philosopher-king', were notably unsuccessful.

Plato's productive life was a long one, stretching from the 390s to his death in 347, and his dialogues are conventionally divided in to three periods, Early, Middle and Late. The broad divisions are largely accepted, although there is much controversy over details, since the dialogues cannot be precisely dated and the exact order of composition is not always certain. We are here concerned with the Early period, the 390s–80s, which saw the composition of mainly short dialogues, in some way presenting conversations held by Socrates with friends and associates – the ones most likely to be related to those of the historical Socrates – in which Socrates asks questions about the nature of values such as piety, bravery, temperance. The order of composition or even approximate dates of these dialogues are unknown, but Plato's account of Socrates' trial speech, the *Apology*, and Socrates' conversation in prison, *Crito*, when he refuses the opportunity to escape offered by his old friend Crito, are likely to be among the earliest.[15] Socrates' death (399 BC) looms over this period of composition, particularly in the long *Gorgias*, which was composed in the early 380s, probably after most of the shorter dialogues and close to Plato's first Sicilian visit, either just before or just after.[16]

Gorgias: an introduction

A preliminary question needs to be asked: why did Plato write dialogues? There were certainly precedents for continuous exposition of philosophical and scientific ideas in the prose treatises of some of the sixth- and fifth-century writers, and this was the medium chosen by Plato's great successor, Aristotle. One possible answer to the question lies in Plato's adoption of the method of his teacher, Socrates, who appears to have believed that real progress in philosophy is made by mutual discussion of issues of importance by two or more individuals, rather than through solitary monologue which appears to have been the main teaching method of the sophists. Right at the beginning of *Gorgias* (447c), Plato presents Socrates as expressing strong preference to discuss rather than hear a display-oration, and this method naturally lends itself to dramatization. It also allows individuals, under questioning and in interaction with others, to examine their own values and assumptions. The pressure of defending beliefs also reveals individual psychology: the emotional and temperamental aspect of personality is for Plato quite as important as the intellectual. In Plato's dialogues people feel ashamed, they needle, insult and tease each other, lose their tempers, joke and express strong feelings of friendship or animosity, as well as engaging in serious intellectual discussion.

The dialogue form also enables Plato to present a vivid picture of social as well as intellectual life in the late fifth century, using venues such as the houses of wealthy and prominent citizens, gymnasia and other public places. We meet distinguished intellectuals such as the sophist Protagoras, dramatists such as Agathon and Aristophanes and politicians such as Nicias and Alcibiades. This is all, of course, Plato's re-creation; trying to work out the dates at which such dramatized meetings are supposed to be taking place reveals multiple inconsistencies (*Gorgias* is a typical example) and we cannot assume strict historical veracity in the presentation of Plato's characters, any more than we can, ultimately, with his Socrates. What does emerge, notably in *Gorgias*, is Plato's perspective on late fifth-century Athenian life and culture from the hindsight of the early fourth, and his presentation of it as a springboard for his own powerfully original ideas.

A third motivation for the dialogue form may have been Plato's ambitious belief that he was, in some sense, taking over the mantle of mainstream Athenian culture. His philosophical ideas represented a radical and usually explicit critique of traditional values, which were expressed in media appropriate to the oral culture Athens still largely was: the poetry of dramatists and the prose of orators and sophists. His 'dramas' preserved the 'face-to-face' presentation, while very consciously rejecting most of the traditional content.

We know nothing about the actual circumstances of composition and dissemination of Plato's dialogues, and so we cannot say for certain whether or not they were actually read aloud or performed, in the Academy or elsewhere; however, the tradition of oral performance, still quite strong in fourth-century Athens, makes this a distinct possibility.

The characters of *Gorgias*

There are, besides Socrates, three main characters in *Gorgias* and they take it in turns to have a dialogue with him. Their importance in the dialogue is in reverse ratio to what we know about them from outside it. The first, Gorgias, is the one whose historical persona we know most about, and who gives his name to the dialogue, although his contribution is the shortest and least significant of the three.[17] He came from the Sicilian city of Leontini and made a grand entrance to Athens in 429 when, as an ambassador for his city, he caught the Athenians' attention with the power of his oratory. We have seen above his claims for the spoken word and how sought after were the skills he professed. The fragmentary remains of his writings suggest that he also developed radical theories casting doubt on whether it was possible to have and communicate knowledge of the external world (as opposed to being able merely to speak about it).[18] Plato's character, on the other hand, does not exhibit any sharpness of intellect; he is presented as a distinguished, even slightly pompous, figure who regularly runs a one-man show in which he claims to be able to answer any question thrown at him (447d), but he soon gets into difficulties with the respectful but probing Socrates.

The second speaker, Polus, who takes over forcefully from Gorgias at 461b3, following an abortive attempt right at the beginning of the dialogue (448a6), was a teacher of rhetoric and pupil of Gorgias, from Acragas in Sicily (the island was an important centre of rhetorical study in the fifth century). We know nothing about Polus outside the pages of Plato; Socrates refers to, and maybe quotes from, a rhetorical work of his. His youthful, volatile personality is, as often in Plato, reflected in his name ('colt' in Greek), and he is handled by Socrates with a degree of sharp, ironic condescension. However, although presented as basically no more intellectually acute than Gorgias, he is more prepared, initially at least, to ignore conventional values, and so allow Socrates to pursue more basic issues related to power and morality.

The third and most important speaker, Callicles, we know

absolutely nothing about historically, even whether he actually existed or is an invention of Plato (his name means something like 'fine reputation').[19] He is presented as a younger member of the Athenian élite embarking on a political career in which surface respect for the democracy covers a more cynical attitude towards political power. He represents the most radical opposition to Socrates in his view that conventional morality is a cover for what he claims is natural justice, in which the strong rule the weak by right. Initially polite to Socrates, he becomes increasingly unsettled and rude in the face of the latter's ability to defeat him in argument and reach what he regards as absurd conclusions. Socrates' insistence that philosophical discussion is not merely a leisure or educational activity for the young, but at the centre of politics and morality, leads their antagonism to the point where Callicles finally refuses to co-operate in the discussion, leaving Socrates to go on alone.

Socrates is obviously the most complex character of the dialogue, and his relationship with the historical person has already been discussed. In the dialogues in general he comes across as an urbane, often ironic questioner of those who advance conventional definitions of moral values (see above) almost always from the position, maintained in his trial speech (e.g. *Apology* 20d ff.), that he was not conscious of knowing anything. What uniquely distinguishes his role in *Gorgias* is how it swiftly develops into a much more assertive, positive stance, which gives a serious and sometimes even an uncharacteristically bitter tone to the dialogue as a whole. In the later stages of the encounter with Callicles, the latter's refusal to co-operate in discussion forces Socrates into a series of long speeches in which he defends his way of life in the face of what he and Callicles both recognize as the impending danger of prosecution for his beliefs.

There is also a minor character, Chaerophon, who takes the stage briefly at the beginning of the dialogue; he was a long-standing and somewhat emotional disciple of Socrates, famous as the man who, according to Plato, questioned the Delphic oracle about whether any man was wiser than Socrates and received a negative answer (*Apology* 21a); he was also a butt of comic dramatists (e.g. Aristophanes in *Clouds*), receiving a nickname 'the bat' from his squeaky voice. We must also not forget an anonymous group of spectators who play a small but vital role in supporting Socrates with clamour in his wish to continue the dialogue with a Gorgias who is displaying signs of polite reluctance when the going starts to get tough (458c3). The presence of an audience adds an edge to the participants' awareness that their discussion is also a public performance.

The issues of the dialogue

The informal start to *Gorgias* gives little warning of what is to follow. As in the shorter dialogues of the Early period, Socrates initiates a series of innocent-sounding questions of someone professing a particular art or skill (Greek *techne*[20]) – in Gorgias' case he wants to pin down the exact nature of his ability to speak persuasively in public, which he has apparently been demonstrating just before Socrates arrives and the dialogue begins. A typical course for the Socratic argument would be attempts at a series of increasingly sophisticated definitions of the art or value the so-called expert professes, ending in more or less good-tempered but perplexed agreement that they have not succeeded in arriving at an acceptable conclusion, but have reached an impasse. In the dialogue, Gorgias claims that his art is persuasion and has as its subject right and wrong (454b). The initial impasse is reached when Socrates picks up Gorgias' admission that his art does not relate to knowledge of this subject, but is only able to produce conviction through persuasion (454e ff.), which contradicts the sophist's claim to be able to teach the subject – an ability, they agree, which comes only through acquiring knowledge of it (460a ff.). *Gorgias* does not stay at this particular level, however, and Socrates does not long maintain his stance of an innocent enquirer. The initial discussion sets the tone for the broad scope and the serious intent of the whole dialogue – to articulate the difference which Socrates perceives between the current practice of orators and teachers of rhetoric, who have a major influence on how states are run (intimately connected with the ability to speak well: see above), and what should, in his opinion, be the real purpose of a human life in society, to live rightly and to achieve ultimate happiness. The dialogue is essentially a radical re-articulation of an idea traditional in Greek ethics, the choice between two lives – of vice and virtue.[21]

Right at the beginning of this Introduction we noted the polarized nature of the discussion, which arises from the radically different basic assumptions of the two sides: Socrates' interlocutors, especially Polus and Callicles, represent in extreme form a 'man in the Agora' view of political life, in which the highest Greek value, 'excellence', is closely associated with personal prestige, power and worldly success, that comes, typically, from the ability to speak well and to persuade people. Socrates believes, on the other hand, that the real politician necessarily aims at the good of the citizens in his charge. Why 'necessarily'? An answer to this question highlights what might, for us, seem strange assumptions on Socrates' part: that a necessary precondition of doing right or good is to know what actually is right and good, i.e. its nature; moreover, the precondition is not only necessary but sufficient: for Plato's Socrates, to know what is right in any given situation is necessarily to do it; and once you really know what is right and good, you cannot want to do wrong. Contemporary tyrants like Archelaus of Macedon and other rulers notorious for wrongdoing are therefore not only injuring others but are actually acting through ignorance of what they really want: in what seems like an almost wilfully paradoxical claim (466d) which amazes and irritates Polus, Socrates maintains that tyrants do not do what they want to, only what they 'decide is best'. Rascally politicians do not really have any power because they are misled about the real ends of their own activity, which must always be to aim at the good.

This is, on first sight, a strange thesis, and we may well find Socrates' line of argument, as Polus, and later Callicles, certainly did, unconvincing – 'monstrous and outrageous' is how Polus puts it, with characteristic bluntness (467b). Power, however exercised, and to whatever end, is still power, since surely what Archelaus decides is best is what he wants to do. And if, as an absolute ruler, he does what he decides, who is to say that he is not, ultimately, happy? Socrates' line of argument may actually have seemed even more peculiar to his contemporaries. It is important, from our perspective, not to import into this discussion notions of doing 'right' and 'good' which assume an altruism in the doer divorced from personal advantage. Socrates' ideal politician is no 'do-gooder' in the modern sense, offering a self-sacrificing alternative to the life of power and prestige and securing happiness that way. Irrespective of what happens to you in a material sense, however much you may suffer physically as a victim of injustice, if you know what the real ends of your activity are – the right and good – you will possess, Socrates maintains, actual power, which is obviously to your advantage. This is what conventional orators and politicians should acquire, but do not.

As far as we are concerned this may deepen rather than resolve the paradox. What is it about knowledge of the good which enables it to confer power on a politician? The answer lies in how Plato's Socrates conceives political activity. He believes that it should be an art like that of the doctor, ship's captain or other professional. An art is an activity which is based on a rationally organized body of knowledge, as opposed to a 'knack' or 'rule of thumb', something which is simply based on experience (*empeiria*: it always seems to work, but the operator does not really know how). In developing this contrast Socrates makes extensive use of the medical analogy: just as the essence of the doctor's skill is to make people healthy, so the excellence of the real politician must be to improve the people he is governing. By 'improve', Socrates does not mean to raise their standard of living or make them successful in war, but to make them better people, just as the doctor knows how to heal the sick. And the issue is much more vital for the politician than the doctor, since, while the task of the latter is merely to heal bodies, the politician should be concerned with people's souls. The Greeks regarded the soul (*psyche*) as that part of the human being which contains the life-force (in the early epic poet Homer, a kind of 'breath'), which leaves the body at death to exist in a ghost-like state in the Underworld. For Plato, however, the soul is much more: it represents the essence of the person, his or her moral value, that part which is affected by the way in which the life of the individual is conducted.

So, only experts – those who professed an art which dealt in knowledge – could effect changes for the better. For Plato's Socrates, oratory is not an art, since, by his own admission, Gorgias does not aim to produce knowledge of right and wrong, but only to persuade – to produce conviction. Instead of aiming at making people better (he cannot, because his art does not include knowledge of right and wrong), he panders to their desires, like a confectioner tempting children.[22] If you engage in pandering you do not have to know what people really need; all you require is experience of what will satisfy them.

Just as the conventional ruler, lacking real knowledge, cannot make his citizens better, he also cannot govern himself. Socrates meets his most serious challenge from the last interlocutor, Callicles, who regards Socrates' thesis as an argument to prevent the powerful from taking their natural place as the rulers of society. Callicles asserts that Socrates' morality is so much nonsense; the powerful have a natural right to dominate the weak and to take from society all that they want in order to satisfy their inner needs. Socrates tries to show Callicles that the unlimited satisfaction of desires is incompatible with political rule, which must depend on the ability to establish an order and proportion not only in society but within oneself. It is only in this way that the individual will be able to acquire the social virtues of temperance, justice towards mortals and reverence towards the gods, and so pass them on to others. This connection of outward behaviour with inner state – the moral and psychological health of the person's soul – is perhaps the most important idea to emerge from the discussion, the more so in being stoutly resisted by Callicles.

As the dialogue reaches its climax it becomes obvious that it is not the foreign tyrant such as Archelaus whom Socrates has primarily in his sights; he is looking nearer home, at the Athenian democracy itself. He claims that not only the budding politician Callicles, but eminent Athenian statesmen of the past, including Themistocles, the hero of the Persian Wars, and Pericles, the architect of the Athenian empire, lack the ruler's art; these eminent men did not aim at the betterment of the citizens in their charge but relied on persuasion to satisfy the desires of those they believed they ruled. Plato's Socrates looks back on the great period of Athenian achievement, which produced the Parthenon and Aeschylus' *Oresteia*, with a jaundiced eye. The provision of an Athenian navy and payment for political services – key manifestations of the power of the democracy without and within – he regards as so much rubbish, merely pandering to the masses.

From this and other dialogues we are made very aware that Plato did not like democracy, and in his perspective on Athenian history in the dialogue we can recognize distortion of the facts resulting from a strong vein of political prejudice.[23] Yet his hostility is not entirely prejudice; he argues that if, as he believes, the right conduct of one's life and the organization of that of others depend on knowledge of what is good, and that knowledge is confined to experts and not within the capability of everyone, then only someone with that knowledge is in a fit state to rule. This implies no ivory tower for the expert in goodness. In a uniquely assertive passage towards the end of the dialogue, Socrates claims (521d6) that he is perhaps the only Athenian 'who studies the true political art'. In a clear reference forwards to his trial (see above) Plato's Socrates connects his refusal to pander to the desires of the Athenians – to tell them what they want to hear – with his likely failure to produce an effective defence in a future prosecution: 'I shall be judged like a doctor brought before a jury of children with a cook as prosecutor' (e3–4). But for Socrates, the danger of the death-penalty is as nothing compared with having to '. . . enter the next world with one's soul loaded with wrongdoing' (522e3–4).

The reference to 'the next world' takes us to the conclusion of the dialogue, in which Socrates relates what he presents as a traditional story (a 'myth') about what happens to the soul after death. How this story fits in with the rest of the dialogue is an issue which will be taken up in the final section; but note here that it enlarges on earlier references to the 'soul' of individuals:

the dead can look forward to the truth about the conduct of their lives being visible to judges in the Underworld through the state of their souls, and rewards and punishment will be meted out accordingly.

Structure and argument

The above account may suggest that Socrates makes all the running, with his interlocutors merely expressing astonishment and outrage, followed by meek agreement or, in Callicles' case, token agreement masking effective withdrawal. So, what is the significance of the dialogue structure? Is it simply a lively, essentially ornamental way of presenting Plato's beliefs, as outlined, through his mouthpiece Socrates, or does the interaction between Socrates and the others contribute something essential to the argument?

It has already been suggested that Plato was interested not just in the dissemination of his philosophy, but in human reactions to it – agreement, disagreement, disbelief, laughter, anger. These reactions are the dynamic which propels forward the transitions in the main tripartite structure of *Gorgias*: Polus bursts in on the conversation with Gorgias (461b3) because he cannot contain his irritation at how they are conducting the argument; in the same way Callicles enters the ring (481b6) when he expresses astonished disbelief at the conclusions reached by Socrates and Polus – is Socrates being serious? But Polus and Callicles do not simply express baffled emotion; each of them puts his finger quite precisely on what he sees as the weakness in the previous argument – the unnecessary concessions which have been made to Socrates and the emotion of shame which prevented a more effective defence: in the case of Polus, what he sees as Gorgias' failure to hold out against Socrates' assertion that the orator must know about and teach right and wrong; and Callicles' similar analysis of Polus' own fatal concession which forced him finally to agree with Socrates that it is better to suffer than to do wrong (for the detailed arguments, see the critical analysis in the Commentary on A[6] and B[5]). In this way we can view Plato criticizing his own argument, as it were, and gradually developing a more formidable challenge to his Socrates through the series of increasingly sophisticated partners in discussion. Each of them rejects the basis of the previous argument, and does so with some heat. Emotion and argument go hand in hand.

Socrates' procedure – which, as he concedes in the *Apology* (23a ff.), aroused considerable exasperation, not to say hostility, in those on whom he practised – is known as the *elenchus*, from the Greek word meaning 'examination', 'questioning'. As a result of questions, he draws an assertion, or agreement to an assertion, from his interlocutor; subsequently, as a result of further questions, the respondent is led to agree to a proposition which contradicts the original assertion. For example: at the very beginning of the dialogue, Socrates asks Gorgias to explain exactly what his art consists in; gradual refinement reveals that his art is speech, and, yet further on, that the subject of his speech is the area of right and wrong, and that he teaches how to persuade on these subjects, but without knowledge. When, however, Gorgias goes on to explain that an orator should, but might not, make a good use of his oratorical skill, Socrates establishes, with Gorgias' agreement, that the expert who knows about right and wrong will never wish to do wrong (460c7), thereby revealing a contradiction with what Gorgias has just asserted. The main point against Gorgias, that since his so-called art is not based on knowledge, it is not an art at all, Socrates postpones to the following section with Polus, possibly to avoid the impression of too brusque a confrontation with the eminent but (in Plato, at least) none too bright Gorgias. Polus suffers a similar fate: having asserted that orators have great power in their cities (466b), he subsequently agrees with Socrates that this cannot be the case; since orators and tyrants do not act from knowledge, they do not do what they really want to do (they are mistaken about their real ends) and so do not have power (468c–d).[24] When Callicles later asserts that it is right that the stronger should have more than the weaker, Socrates draws him into a series of inconsistencies by questioning him over what he actually means by 'stronger' (C[3]).

All three interlocutors react to this questioning of their cherished beliefs with emotions ranging from mild mystification (Gorgias) to amazed irritation (Polus) to real antagonism (Callicles). Plato's Socrates, however, continually insists that his purpose is not to win the argument (the practice of dispute, associated with the sophists), but to discover the truth by means of co-operative discussion with the interlocutor (through dialectic). It is only by this form of face-to-face discussion that the truth will emerge.[25] An important point which Socrates emphasizes on several occasions in *Gorgias* is that agreement between him and his interlocutor means far more than the unargued authority of others, however many they are and however eminent (B[4]). Socrates claims that he can pull in anybody off the street, no matter how obscure they are, in order to have an effective discussion to get at the truth on any given subject (though in Plato's dialogues his associates tend to be professional and/or upper-class).

There is, however, an important proviso: the collaborator must say what he sincerely believes; he must not let *amour propre* or other emotions force him to reply to Socrates insincerely. This is the downfall of Callicles, who reacts to Socrates' successful probing first with anger and scorn, then with answers in which he claims he is 'going along' with Socrates in order to bring the discussion to a close and to oblige Gorgias (501c), and finally, with virtual silence, forcing Socrates to go on alone. The *elenchus* is therefore not just a test of intellect but of character – willingness to admit weaknesses as well as strengths.

But does Plato's Socrates himself ever reveal any weaknesses? He tells Gorgias (A[5]) that he is more than willing to have his own mistakes pointed out to him – he says that in fact he prefers to be on the receiving end. Yet this never happens to any effect; the only opposition to Socrates takes the form of unargued 'man-in-the-street' views, which he invariably refutes, even persuading (or in Callicles' case, trying to persuade) his interlocutors that these original assertions do not even represent what they really believe themselves, once he is able to lead them to the truth.

This leaves one major problem with Socrates' method: demonstrating that your opponents hold inconsistent or contradictory beliefs does not necessarily entail the truth of those that you are asserting, even if, as in *Gorgias*, you manage to persuade your fellow-speakers to agree with you most of the time. What does not go under scrutiny in *Gorgias*, or elsewhere in Plato, is the validity of the method itself, which appears to deliver consistency rather than truth.[26] In the course of the dialogue, Socrates asserts, and ultimately gets agreement on, a number of propositions which many would find it difficult to agree with: that oratory is not an art;[27] that being good and just, i.e. pursuing the good life, is a question of expert knowledge; that those who do wrong have no power and cannot ultimately be happy; that it is better to suffer than to do wrong. These propositions are sometimes assumed to be true, for example, the idea that being good, etc., is a matter of knowledge is assumed by analogy with expertise in other activities, such as music and medicine (see 460b–c); or the positions are supported with arguments which, as we shall see, are often quite complex, but contain steps which, while they seem to get the assent of Socrates' interlocutors, do not always satisfy us. In some cases we might even find that we may agree with Socrates' conclusion, but not with the steps he takes to get there (see, e.g., Commentary on B[5] and C[5]). And, in the end, Socrates cannot, by this method, force his interlocutors to agree with him, however clear and decisive his logic may appear to be, as Callicles demonstrates. There are signs in *Gorgias* that Plato was beginning to recognize that the *elenchus* had its limitations.

Socrates and the 'good life'

In reading *Gorgias* it is important to remember, obvious as it may seem, that we are not witnessing a live debate; all the words are those of the author of the dialogue. Plato is in control of everything which his characters say, how they behave and the outcome of every argument. In staging the debate the author clearly has certain aims in mind, the overriding one being to examine how a person should live: whether the choice should be the pursuit of goodness and justice or of illusory power and satisfaction of material wants. Plato feels the importance of this choice so acutely that, in a sense, his justification for the good life is largely independent of the detailed arguments apparently supporting it; for example, the introduction of the soul as the part of the individual containing his or her moral essence (477a7) largely supersedes the slightly dodgy chain of reasoning by which Socrates seeks to convince Polus that 'it is better to suffer than to do wrong'; if suffering wrong is better for the soul than doing wrong, just as, by analogy, health is self-evidently better for the body than sickness, what more needs to be said? Likewise, in the long debate with Callicles C[1–12]) the argumentation finishes essentially at 506c4 (the end of C[7]). For the rest of the dialogue, Callicles is a token, or sulky presence, while Socrates embarks on a series of speeches justifying his choice of how to live. On a dramatic level, Socrates has been forced by Callicles' non-cooperation into abandoning the *elenchus* and making long speeches (*makrologia*), a procedure which he customarily deprecates, and for which he apologizes to the assembled company. Structurally, however, such a change in method reflects the seriousness of the subject: Socrates' arguments have been made; now is the time for Plato to present a more personal justification of his master's life. Gone is the humour and raillery of the earlier arguments. How one should live really is a matter of life and death – for Socrates personally as well as for others. The allusions to Socrates' own fate at the hands of the Athenian court cast a long shadow over the final sections of the work.

The very final section of *Gorgias* (C[12]) departs radically from the structure of the rest of the dialogue, consisting of the telling by Socrates of a myth, a narrative about what happens to the souls of humans when they die.[28] Although presented by Socrates as 'the truth' (523a3), it appears to derive its validation from a different source: from the authority of tradition rather than that of logic. We should not exaggerate the difference: Socrates has been using images from Greek myth and legend throughout the dialogue to illustrate his arguments, for example the story of Amphion the musician and Zethus the herdsman, representing the life of personal contemplation versus political ambition, dramatized in Euripides' largely lost tragedy *Antiope* (484e), or the fate of intemperate souls in the afterlife representing the evil consequences of excess (493a ff.). This is all part of the strongly 'protreptic' aspect of the later stages of the dialogue, i.e. the element of moral exhortation as opposed to argument; Plato doubtless wishes to commend his radical philosophical conclusions as in some sense deriving their authority from tradition.[29]

These are all, however, to a greater or lesser extent, examples quoted by way of analogy or reinforcement of a truth independently established in the main arguments of *Gorgias*. The question that a modern audience is likely to ask about the final myth is whether, rather than reinforcing, it actually replaces the argument; or, in other words, is Socrates' 'good life' really being lived principally in order to ensure a 'good death'? Is the condition of the soul at death, when the individual comes naked before the gods of the Underworld for judgement, the main preoccupation? And, if so, what of all those arguments in *Gorgias* that attempt to prove the worth of the good life for itself in the here and now? If the judgement in the afterlife is what life here is all about, keeping one's soul unmarred by wrongdoing would seem to be no more than a prudent precaution to avoid an ultimate fate as grim as it is unavoidable.

Put like this, the question is difficult to answer; but perhaps our 'either/or' is not the right way to pose the question. Plato and his audience may not have conceived the two forms of discourse as mutually exclusive; the myth can perhaps be seen as presenting a complementary rather than an alternative authority for Plato's central truth about human life, as it does in the other similar myths which conclude the later dialogues, *Phaedo* and *Republic*.

It would be a mistake, however, I think, to read into the ending of *Gorgias* the serenity with which Plato's Socrates concludes those later dialogues; in *Phaedo* (115 ff.) he goes untroubled, in marked contrast to his audience, to his death, and his exposition of the afterlife in *Republic* (614b ff.) is the culmination of a wide-ranging and detailed exposition of Plato's ideal state, his Utopia. In *Gorgias*, which looks in many ways like an early sketch for *Republic*, the argument is anchored very much in this world, and we finish in the dark as to whether

Socrates has really persuaded his audience of what he values most. What has Callicles (or the others, for that matter) to say in reply to the myth? We have no way of knowing, since, unlike *Phaedo*, there is no 'frame' to the dialogue, no narrator who can explain or comment, and no audience whose acquiescence can be assumed, as in *Republic*. We just have Socrates' last words (527e): 'let us follow that way [practising righteousness and virtue] and urge others to follow it, instead of the way which you in mistaken confidence are urging upon me; for that way is worthless, Callicles.' This stark, uncompromising ending suggests that the absence of narrator may be an important factor in Plato's design; he may wish to avoid the softening effect of narrative mediation in dramatizing Socrates' lack of success in creating empathy with his interlocutors, his inability to teach them about goodness and justice, which, ironically enough, seems in danger of putting him in the same camp as all the failed statesmen he criticizes.

The significance may be broader; it has already been pointed out that the shadow of the Athenian trial and condemnation of Socrates falls long over the later sections of the dialogue. Gorgias, Polus and Callicles may represent an audience of all those prominent Athenians whose reactions to Socrates' words led to his downfall. Writing within fifteen or so years of Socrates' execution, Plato may be attempting to keep the sharp edges of his memory alive and to create for his contemporaries a dramatic image of what Socrates' life, with its blend of success and heroic failure, meant for his pupil.

NOTES

1. In the Platonic tradition, probably already in the Alexandrian period (3rd–1st centuries BC), a hundred or so years after Plato's death, the dialogue acquired a sub-title *Gorgias, or on Oratory*. It was the most admired of Plato's dialogues in the rhetorically based culture of later Antiquity (1st–4th centuries AD).
2. *Encomium of Helen* 12 (MacDowell 1982).
3. As Thucydides has Pericles boast in the Funeral Speech over the

Athenian war dead in 431 BC (*History of the Peloponnesian War* 2.40).

4. For the distinction Plato makes between sophists and orators, see *Gorgias* 520b.
5. See *Antigone* 441 ff.
6. The author is either the well-known tragedian Euripides or the sophist Critias.
7. See Aristophanes, *Clouds* 112 ff.
8. Thucydides 5.105 (tr. R. Warner).
9. For explanation of Greek value-terms, see Glossary of Greek Terms.
10. Plato, *Apology* 30e ff.
11. On Alcibiades, see *Gorgias* 481d2 and note.
12. Plato does not feature himself in any dialogue, with two minor exceptions: in *Apology* 34a Socrates mentions him as being present in court during the trial, and in the last meeting between Socrates and his associates in prison before he drinks the hemlock, the narrator Phaedo mentions that Plato was, he believes, ill on that day (*Phaedo* 59b).
13. Collected in Giannantoni 1994. See also Clay 1994.
14. Plato, *Letter VII*, 325d ff., in *Phaedrus and Letters VII & VIII*, tr. W. Hamilton (Harmondsworth: Penguin Classics, 1973), p. 114.
15. On the other hand, *Phaedo*, the dialogue which leads up to his actual death, although grouped in, for example, the Penguin Classics series in a volume entitled *The Last Days of Socrates* (tr. Hugh Tredennick, ed. Harold Tarrant; Harmondsworth, 1993), is clearly, in view of the philosophical doctrines introduced there, a later composition from Plato's Middle period.
16. For a different view of the order of the early dialogues, see Kahn 1996, and for a discussion of the date of composition of *Gorgias* and its relationship to the Sicilian visit, see Guthrie 1975, pp. 284–5, and Dodds 1959, pp. 18–30.
17. Many of Plato's dialogues are named after a (or the) major participant, with Socrates, although we don't know for certain if these titles are Plato's or have their origin at a later period; Gorgias is certainly not the major participant in *Gorgias*, although undoubtedly the best known after Socrates (then, as well as now), and his initial claims for the power of oratory in some sense epitomize the main issues at stake in the dialogue as a whole.
18. On the doctrines of Gorgias, see Waterfield 2000, pp. 222–40, and Kerferd 1981, pp. 78–82.

19. Dodds 1959, pp. 12–13, takes the view that Callicles was a real person, from the circumstantial detail that Plato gives him a *deme* (district of origin in Athens) and at one point mentions the name of his lover (who was a historical person) and three of his friends. Dodds speculates on the reasons why there is no other mention of Callicles: it is possible that, as an outspoken and ambitious politician, he died young in the political and military chaos at the end of the Peloponnesian War (see *Gorgias* 519a7).
20. For the meaning of *techne*, see A Note on the Text; the word will be rendered as 'art' in the Introduction from this point on.
21. The god Heracles (according to the sophist Prodicus, quoted by Socrates in Xenophon, *Memoirs of Socrates* 2.1.21–34), when approaching manhood, was confronted by two goddesses, Vice and Virtue, between whose persuasion he was obliged to choose.
22. An image from *Gorgias* (521e ff.). This argument seems tailor-made for application to the modern advertising industry; does it pander to unnecessary and unhealthy desires, as Plato would surely maintain, or allow people opportunities profitably to enhance their lives?
23. For the details, see Commentary on C[10].
24. For the close connection of oratory with political power at Athens, see 'The cultural background', above.
25. In a later dialogue, *Phaedrus*, Socrates emphasizes the superiority of interactive speech over writing as a method of investigating philosophical questions (274 ff.).
26. On this fundamental weaknesses of the method of *elenchus*, see Vlastos 1983.
27. In the ancient world, rhetoric was popularly regarded as an art or skill *par excellence*, which would have made Socrates' assertion appear even more paradoxical to his original audience than it does, perhaps, to us.
28. For details, see Commentary and notes on C[12].
29. Just as his striking images, e.g. of the modest skipper (C[9]), are intended, rather like parables, to reinforce his philosophical conclusions from 'real life'. Socrates is continually being chided for his addiction to images and examples from humble activities and professions, e.g. by Callicles at 491a1.

Further Reading

Comprehensive bibliography on Plato by L. Brisson and H. Ioannidi (containing index directions to detailed studies of *Gorgias*), covering the years 1958 to 1990, can be found in the bibliographical publication *Lustrum* (Göttingen, Vandenhoek and Ruprecht) as follows:

'Platon 1958–1975', *Lustrum* 20 (1977), pp. 5–304;
'Platon 1975–1980', *Lustrum* 25 (1983), pp. 31–320;
'Platon 1980–1985', *Lustrum* 30 (1988), pp. 11–294;
'Platon 1985–1990', *Lustrum* 34 (1992), pp. 1–338.

See also *L'Année Philologique* (under 'Plato Philosophus'), a year-by-year bibliography of Classical Antiquity.

The following represents a short selection of the most significant and approachable editions, translations and secondary literature.

Texts, commentaries and translations

Burnet, J., *Platonis Opera*, 5 vols. (Oxford: Oxford University Press, 1903): the standard Greek text of Plato (vol. 3 contains *Gorgias*).

Dodds, E. R., *Gorgias, a Revised Text with Introduction and Commentary* (Oxford: Oxford University Press, 1959; Sandpiper reprinted 2001): the most important modern commentary on the Greek text of *Gorgias*, containing a thorough revision of the text based on re-examination of the manuscript tradition.

Irwin, T., *Plato: Gorgias, Translated with Notes* (Oxford: Oxford University Press, 1979): a deliberately literal translation with an advanced philosophical commentary.

Waterfield, R., *Plato: Gorgias; Translated with Introduction and Notes* (Oxford: Oxford University Press, Oxford World Classics, 1994): a lively, idiomatic translation, with useful commentary, especially on the detail of philosophical issues.

Zeyl, D. J., *Plato; Gorgias, Translated with Introduction and Notes* (Indianapolis: Hackett, 1987).

There are three collections of translations of the complete works of Plato which contain *Gorgias*:

Allen, R. E., *The Dialogues of Plato*, 4 vols. (New Haven: Yale University Press, 1984): vol. 1 contains *Gorgias*.

Cooper, J., *Plato's Complete* Works (Indianapolis: Hackett, 1997).

Hamilton, E. and Cairns, H., *The Complete Dialogues of Plato* (New Jersey: Princeton University Press, 1961).

The cultural and intellectual background

Buxton, R. G. A., *Persuasion in Greek Tragedy: A Study of 'Peitho'* (Cambridge: Cambridge University Press, 1982).

Clay, D., 'The origins of the Socratic Dialogue', in P. A. Vander Waerdt (ed.), *The Socratic Movement* (Ithaca/London: Cornell University Press, 1994), pp. 23–47.

Dover, K. J., *Greek Popular Morality in the Time of Plato and Aristotle* (Oxford: Blackwell, 1974; reprinted with corrections, Indianapolis/Cambridge: Hackett, 1994): a detailed examination of the popular use of ethical language in the literature contemporary with Plato.

Giannantoni, G., *Socratis et Socraticorum Reliquiae*, 4 vols. (2nd edition; Naples: Edizioni dell' Ateneo, 1994): a full edition of the fragmentary texts of the writers, other than Plato, associated with Socrates (see Clay above).

Guthrie, W. K. C., *A History of Greek Philosophy*, Vol. 3: *The Fifth-Century Enlightenment* (Cambridge: Cambridge

University Press, 1969): the standard detailed cultural history of the sophists and Socrates. Also available in two parts: *The Sophists* and *Socrates*.

Kerferd, G., *The Sophistic Movement* (Cambridge: Cambridge University Press, 1981).

MacDowell, D. M., *Gorgias: Encomium of Helen, Edited with Introduction, Notes and Translation* (Bristol: Bristol Classical Press, 1982).

Waterfield, R., *The First Philosophers: The Presocratics and Sophists, Translated with Commentary* (Oxford: Oxford University Press, Oxford World Classics, 2000).

Plato (general)

Guthrie, W. K. C., *A History of Greek Philosophy*, Vol. 4: *Plato: The Man and his Dialogues, Earlier Period* (Cambridge: Cambridge University Press, 1975): a detailed survey of all the dialogues up to and including *Republic*.

Hare, R. M., *Plato* (Oxford: Oxford University Press, 1982): a short general survey.

Irwin, T., *Classical Thought* (Oxford: Oxford University Press, 1989): chs. 5 and 6 give a succinct basic and approachable summary of Plato's thought.

—, *Plato's Ethics* (Oxford: Oxford University Press, 1995): a detailed and advanced account of Plato's moral thought.

Kraut, R. (ed.), *The Cambridge Companion to Plato* (Cambridge: Cambridge University Press, 1992): a collection of articles on all aspects of Plato's thought.

Vlastos, G., *Socrates, Ironist and Moral Philosopher* (Cambridge: Cambridge University Press, 1991): a series of detailed essays on specific aspects of the thought of Plato's Socrates, including an attempt to separate 'Socratic' from 'Platonic' thought (chs. 2 and 3).

Studies relating to *Gorgias*

Annas, J., 'Plato's myths of judgement', *Phronesis* 27 (1982), pp. 119–43: this article contains discussion of the myth at the end of *Gorgias* in the context of Plato's other eschatological myths.

Beversluis, J., *Cross-examining Socrates: a Defense of the Interlocutors in Plato's Early Dialogues* (Cambridge: Cambridge University Press, 2000): contains detailed chapters (pp. 291–376) considering the arguments from the point of view of Gorgias, Polus and Callicles.

Kahn, C. H., 'Drama and dialectic in Plato's *Gorgias*', *Oxford Studies in Ancient Philosophy* 1 (1983), pp. 75–121: a study which is important for its emphasis on the emotional and intellectual elements in the exchanges between Socrates and his interlocutors in *Gorgias*.

—, *Plato and the Socratic Dialogue: The Philosophical Use of a Literary Form* (Cambridge: Cambridge University Press, 1996): see especially ch. 5 on *Gorgias*, which, Kahn argues, was composed before most of the other Early dialogues as a 'foundational text'.

Kaufmann, C., 'Enactment as argument in *Gorgias*', *Philosophy and Rhetoric* 12 (1979), pp. 114–29: the author argues that in this dialogue Plato's Socrates uses rhetoric negatively in order to draw attention to its limitations.

Klosko, G., 'The refutation of Callicles in Plato's *Gorgias*', *Greece and Rome* 31(2), (1984), pp. 126–39: an examination of the treatment of Callicles' hedonistic thesis in the last section of the dialogue.

Lewis, T. J., 'Refutative rhetoric as true rhetoric in the *Gorgias*', *Interpretation* 14 (1986), pp. 195–210: particularly interesting in this article is the emphasis the author gives to the social 'performing' context of the dialogue.

Nightingale, A. W., *Genres in Dialogue: Plato and the Construct of Philosophy* (Cambridge: Cambridge University Press, 1995): ch. 2 ('Use and abuse of Greek tragedy') examines in detail Plato's use in *Gorgias* of Euripides' *Antiope* as a parallel to the argument between Socrates and Callicles (see *Gorgias* C[1] below).

Santas, G. X., *Socrates' Philosophy in Plato's Early Dialogues* (London: Routledge, 1979): ch. 8 ('Power, virtue and happiness') has a long detailed section on the arguments of *Gorgias*.

Scott, D., 'Platonic pessimism and moral education', *Oxford Studies in Ancient Philosophy* 17 (1999), pp. 15–36: a discussion of the limitations of the *elenchus* in *Gorgias* and *Republic*.

Vlastos, G., 'Was Polus refuted?', *American Journal of Philology* 88 (1967), pp. 454–60: an article which questions the validity of Socrates' reasoning in the discussion with Polus (on this see also Beversluis, Kahn 1983 and Santas above).

—, 'The Socratic elenchus', *Oxford Studies in Ancient Philosophy* 1 (1983), pp. 27–58 and 71–4 (replying to comments on the article by R. Kraut, pp. 59–70): an incisive discussion of the relationship between Plato's dialectic and the establishment of truth.

Woolf, R., 'Callicles and Socrates: psychic (dis)harmony in the *Gorgias*', *Oxford Studies in Ancient Philosophy* 18 (2000), pp. 1–40.

A Note on the Text

The translation is based on that of Walter Hamilton for the first Penguin edition (1960 and reprints). It has, however, been reworked throughout, using the Oxford Text of J. Burnet (1903), supplemented by E. R. Dodds (1959); I refrain from discussing disputed textual points in the Notes, except on a few occasions where they have significance for the meaning. While attempting to retain the smoothness and readability of Hamilton, I have tried, by keeping closer to the Greek, to convey more of the directness, even bluntness, of the argumentative exchanges between Socrates and his interlocutors. I have also preferred to retain the Greek forms for exclamations, for example 'By Hera!' (for Hamilton's 'My word!'), even when they may sound odd in English, such as Socrates' favourite 'By the dog!'.

How to translate Greek value-terms is always a problematic issue; I have chosen to follow Hamilton in generally rendering *dikaios* and *adikos* (literally, 'just' and 'unjust') as, more broadly, 'right' and 'wrong' (for an explanation, see Notes, n. 17), except where a legal context of argument makes the narrower literal meaning more appropriate, for example 476b. On the other hand, I have regularly altered 'blessed' (for *agathos*) into the more literal 'good'; however undefined this may sound (and arguably it remains vague in Greek), it avoids the danger of anachronistic religious associations. I have retained Hamilton's 'art' for the key term *techne*. 'Skill' or 'craft' are common alternative renderings, and these may convey more of the idea of rational procedure which Plato wishes to give the word; however, the common modern associations of 'skill' or 'craft' tend to be much narrower than the Greek, and rather misleading in the context. 'Art' is not ideal but is, I think, the best rendering available. For the range of meaning of some key Greek terms frequently used in *Gorgias*, see the Glossary of Greek Terms.

Gorgias

A: DIALOGUE WITH GORGIAS 447a1–461b2

A[1] 447a1–449c8

The dialogue is in direct speech (and not reported second or third hand as with some Platonic dialogues). The setting is a gymnasium or similar building where the celebrated orator Gorgias has been lecturing (despite Callicles' invitation at 447b7, it appears that the participants never do reach his house). There is also an unspecified audience of bystanders (see 458b5 ff.). The introduction is very brief, and Socrates, initially aided by his associate Chaerophon, soon gets down to the main business of this section of the dialogue, an attempt to pin down what Gorgias' art (techne) *consists of – 'What sort of man he is' (447d1), in the way other professionals can be called, for example, shoemakers, doctors or painters. It is established that Gorgias' art is oratory.*

The dialogue in this and subsequent sections is accompanied by typically vivid and humorous characterization: Gorgias' complacent, even pompous, self-assurance at 448a1–2 and 449c1–7 is contrasted with Polus' abrupt and rash attempt to take over Gorgias' role in the conversation at 448a6 (his name means 'colt' in Greek). However, the sharply observed portraits, which emerge through the exchanges, introduce a serious point of major significance for the course of the dialogue as a whole: the normal professional practice of both Gorgias and Polus is to deliver an elaborate 'display-speech' (epideixis)*, either spontaneously or in answer to questions, and this is what they think will be appropriate here; but what Socrates wants is to 'converse', i.e. have a conversation or dialogue* (dialegesthai)*.*

He wants not mere description or praise of Gorgias' art (as in Polus' sample at 448c4 ff.), but to be told what exactly it is. The discussion form Socrates typically adopts in the dialogues is an elenchus *('scrutiny', 'questioning for purposes of refutation'). By means of answers (usually) to his questions, both Socrates and his associate in the discussion proceed by a series of steps to mutually agreed conclusions. The 'refutation' usually consists in Socrates' associate being shown that the result of the discussion is an assertion which contradicts his original position or leads to absurdity, as happens on numerous occasions in* Gorgias.

447 CALLICLES: Your arrival, Socrates, is the kind they recommend for a war or a battle.

SOCRATES: Are you implying that, in the proverbial phrase, we are late for a feast?[1]

CALLICLES: You are indeed, and a very elegant feast too. Gorgias has just finished displaying all manner of fine things to us.

SOCRATES: Well, Chaerephon here is to blame for this, Callicles; he made us linger in the market-place.

b CHAEREPHON: Never mind, Socrates, I'll put the matter right. Gorgias is a friend of mine and will give us a display, now, if you like, or, if you prefer, at some other time.

CALLICLES: Is Socrates really keen to hear Gorgias, Chaerephon?

CHAEREPHON: This is exactly what we are here for.

CALLICLES: Then come home with me whenever you want, for Gorgias is staying with me, and will, I am sure, put on a display for you.

SOCRATES: Splendid, Callicles, but would he be willing to c enter into conversation with us? I want to ask him what the power of his art consists in and what it is that he professes and teaches. The display can wait for some other time, as you say.

CALLICLES: There is nothing like asking the man himself, Socrates. As a matter of fact, one of the features of his display just now was an invitation to anyone in the house to ask what questions he liked, accompanied by a promise to answer them all.

SOCRATES: Excellent news. Ask him, Chaerephon.

CHAEREPHON: Ask him what?

SOCRATES: What sort of man he is. d

CHAEREPHON: What do you mean?[2]

SOCRATES: Well, if he happened to be a manufacturer of shoes, for example, he would presumably answer that he was a shoemaker. Now do you understand?

CHAEREPHON: Perfectly. I'll ask him. Tell me, Gorgias, is Callicles here speaking the truth when he says that you profess to answer any question that is put to you?

GORGIAS: Yes, Chaerephon. That is precisely what I claimed 448 just now, and I may say that no one has put a new question to me for many years.

CHAEREPHON: Then you will doubtless have no difficulty in answering, Gorgias.

GORGIAS: Try and see, Chaerephon.

POLUS: Try, by Zeus, but on me if you please, Chaerephon. Gorgias is worn out, I'm sure, after all that he has just been through.

CHAEREPHON: What's this, Polus? Do you think that you could answer better than Gorgias?

POLUS: What difference does that make, as long as my answer b satisfies you?

CHAEREPHON: No difference at all. Do the answering then, since you want to.

POLUS: Put your question.

CHAEREPHON: Here it is, then. If Gorgias were an expert in the same art as his brother Herodicus, what would be the right name to give him? The same as his brother, presumably?

POLUS: Of course.

CHAEREPHON: Then it would be fair for us to call him a doctor?

POLUS: Yes.

CHAEREPHON: But if his art were the same as that of Aristophon, the son of Aglaophon, or *his* brother,[3] what would be the correct title to give him then?

US: A painter, obviously.

HAEREPHON: Well then, what is the art in which Gorgias is expert, and what would we rightly call him?

POLUS: There are a number of arts, Chaerephon, which men have discovered empirically as a result of experience; for it is experience that enables our span of life to proceed according to art, whereas lack of experience leaves us at the mercy of chance. Different men practise different arts in different ways, but the best men practise the best arts. Gorgias is one of these, and the art which he practises is the finest of them all.[4]

d SOCRATES: I see, Gorgias, that Polus is endowed with a splendid gift of eloquence, but he isn't doing what he promised Chaerephon.

GORGIAS: What do you mean exactly, Socrates?

SOCRATES: As far as I can see, he is not quite answering the question.

GORGIAS: Well, ask him yourself then, if you like.

SOCRATES: Not if you would consent to answer it personally; I would much rather question you. From what he has said it is clear to me that Polus has devoted himself much more to what is called oratory than to the art of conversation.

e POLUS: Why do you say that, Socrates?

SOCRATES: Because, Polus, when Chaerephon asks you what art Gorgias has knowledge of, you embark on a panegyric of his art as if someone were attacking it, without, however, saying what it is.

POLUS: Didn't I say that it was the finest?

SOCRATES: Certainly. But no one is asking how you would describe Gorgias' art but what it *is* and what Gorgias should 449 be called. Just answer these questions now in the same excellent and concise way you did the questions which Chaerephon put to you at first: what is Gorgias' art and what ought we to call him. Or better still, tell us yourself, Gorgias, in what art you are expert and what in consequence we ought to call you.

GORGIAS: My art is oratory, Socrates.

SOCRATES: Then we ought to call you an orator?

GORGIAS: Yes, and a good one, if you want to call me what, in Homer's phrase, 'I boast myself to be'.[5]

SOCRATES: That is exactly what I do want.

GORGIAS: Then call me that.

SOCRATES: Then are we to say that you can make others what you are yourself? b

GORGIAS: That is precisely what I profess to do at Athens and elsewhere.

SOCRATES: Would you be willing then, Gorgias, to continue the discussion on the present lines, by way of question and answer, and to put off to another occasion the kind of long continuous discourse that Polus was embarking on? Be true to your promise, and show yourself willing to give brief answers to what you are asked.

GORGIAS: Some answers, Socrates, necessarily require a speech of some length. But all the same I will try to be as brief as c possible. As a matter of fact, one of the claims I make is that nobody can express a given idea more concisely than I.

SOCRATES: Just what is needed, Gorgias. Give me a display of your talent for brevity and let your discursive style wait for another occasion.

GORGIAS: Certainly, and you will admit that you have never heard anyone more concise.

A[2] 449c9–451d4

Having established Gorgias' profession, Socrates probes further. His questions attempt to narrow down the precise object of Gorgias' art, i.e. what it is knowledge of, by trying to pinpoint what makes the function of oratory unique, as opposed to that of other arts. When it has been established that, unlike arts where speech simply plays a part, e.g. medicine or physical training, oratory is entirely concerned with speech, Socrates then introduces a further distinction: what distinguishes oratory from other arts ostensibly in the same category, e.g. arithmetic or astronomy? These arts are conducted more or less entirely through speech and have objects of knowledge (number, movements of the heavenly bodies). What is the corresponding object of oratory?

SOCRATES: Come then: you say that you understand the art of oratory and can make orators of others. Whatever is the object d with which oratory is concerned? Weaving, for example, is concerned with the production of clothes, is it not?

GORGIAS: Yes.

SOCRATES: And music with the creation of melodies?

GORGIAS: Yes.

SOCRATES: By Hera,[6] Gorgias, I marvel at your answers; they certainly are as short as can be.

GORGIAS: Yes, I think I'm pretty good at brevity, Socrates.

SOCRATES: You are indeed. So, come then, answer me now in the same way about oratory as well. What is it that oratory is the knowledge of?

e GORGIAS: Speech.

SOCRATES: What sort of speech, Gorgias? The kind which tells the sick how they must live in order to get well?

GORGIAS: No.

SOCRATES: Then oratory is not concerned with every kind of speech?

GORGIAS: Certainly not.

SOCRATES: And yet it makes men good at[7] speaking?

GORGIAS: Yes.

SOCRATES; And presumably, good too at thinking about the subjects on which it teaches them to speak?[8]

GORGIAS: Of course.

450 SOCRATES: Now, does medicine, which we mentioned just now, make men good at thinking and speaking about the sick?

GORGIAS: Necessarily.

SOCRATES: So it appears that medicine too is concerned with speech?

GORGIAS: Yes.

SOCRATES: Speech about ailments?

GORGIAS: Of course.

SOCRATES: Similarly, physical training[9] is concerned with speech about the fitness of our bodies and the opposite?

GORGIAS: Undoubtedly.

SOCRATES: And the same is true about all the other arts,

Gorgias. Each of them is concerned with the kind of speech that is relevant to the subject with which that particular art deals. b

GORGIAS: So it seems.

SOCRATES: Then, since you call whatever art is concerned with speech oratory, why do you not call the other arts oratory, seeing that they are admittedly concerned with speech?

GORGIAS: Because, Socrates, whereas with the other arts the knowledge appropriate to them is almost wholly concerned with manual operations and such like, there is nothing analogous in the case of oratory, which does its work and produces its effect entirely by means of speech. That is why I assert that c the art of oratory is the art of speech *par excellence*, and I maintain that I am right.

SOCRATES: I am not sure that I understand what sort of character you mean to give to oratory, but I shall soon know more clearly. Answer me this – we recognize the existence of arts, do we not?

GORGIAS: Yes.

SOCRATES: Now, among all the arts, there are, I think, some which consist mainly of action and have little or no need of speech, arts such as painting and sculpture and many others, which could be carried on in silence. It is with arts such as these, I suppose, that you say that oratory has no concern, am I right? d

GORGIAS: Absolutely right, Socrates.

SOCRATES: But there are other arts which achieve their whole effect by speech, and have no need of action – or very little – arithmetic, for example, and calculation[10] and geometry and I would add games like backgammon[11] and so on. In some of them speech and action play almost equal parts, but in many speech is the more important and is entirely responsible for the whole business and its result. It is in this class that you e place oratory, I think?

GORGIAS: Certainly.

SOCRATES: But I don't believe that you really mean to call any of these arts oratory, though you actually asserted that the art achieving its effect through speech is oratory, and anybody wanting to quibble might retort: 'So Gorgias, you are calling arithmetic oratory?' Yet I don't suppose that you would call either arithmetic or geometry oratory.

451 GORGIAS: You are quite right not to suppose so, Socrates.

SOCRATES: Well then, finish your answer to the question which I was asking you. If oratory is one of those arts which chiefly employ speech and there are other arts in the same class, try to say what is the subject about which oratory achieves its effects in speech. For example, if someone were to ask me about one or other of the arts which I mentioned just now, b 'Tell me, Socrates, what is the art of arithmetic?' I should reply, as you just did, that it is one of the arts which achieves its results by means of speech. And if he were to go on to ask, 'Speech about what?', I should say about odd and even numbers of whatever magnitude. If he were then to ask, 'What do you mean by the art of calculation?', I should answer that this too is one of the class which achieves its whole result by means of speech. And if he asked me again: 'Speech about c what?', I should say, like those who draft amendments for the assembly, that except in one point what we have said of arithmetic may stand,[12] calculation and arithmetic both being concerned with the same subject, odd and even; calculation, however, differs this much: that it contemplates the magnitude of odd and even numbers relatively to one and another as well as absolutely. And if in reply to a question about astronomy I said that this too does its whole work by means of speech, and were then asked, 'Speech about what is astronomy's concern, Socrates?', I should reply, 'About the movements of the stars and the sun and moon and their relative speeds.'

GORGIAS: A very good answer, Socrates.

d SOCRATES: Then you too follow my example, Gorgias. Isn't oratory one of those arts which accomplish their work and purpose entirely through speech?

GORGIAS: It is.

A[3] 451d5–454c6

Gorgias repeats Polus' procedure (448c4 ff. above) of answering Socrates' question by praising his art but not saying what its object is. Socrates quotes a popular song to emphasize his point: how would Gorgias maintain the value of the object of his art in the face of competition from other professionals? This finally produces an answer – the object of oratory (the 'good' it produces) is to persuade people. Socrates then proceeds to extract from Gorgias a further vital distinction: other arts produce conviction too; what does oratory produce conviction about? Answer: conviction in front of large public gatherings about right and wrong.

SOCRATES: Then tell me its subject. Whatever is it that forms the subject of this speech which oratory employs?

GORGIAS: The greatest and best of human concerns, Socrates.

SOCRATES: But even this answer, Gorgias, is open to dispute [e] and far from clear. You have heard, I suppose, people at parties singing the well-known song where they count up the best things: asserting that the greatest good is health, the next beauty, and the third, according to the author of the song, wealth honestly come by?[13]

GORGIAS: Of course I have heard it. But what is your point here?

SOCRATES: Suppose you had standing before you all at once [452] the producers of the good things praised by the author of the song, the doctor and the trainer and the man of business. Take the doctor first. He might say, 'Gorgias is deceiving you, Socrates; it is my art, not his, that deals with man's greatest good.' If I then ask him: 'Who are you to talk like this?', he will answer, I suppose, that he is a doctor. 'What do you mean then? Is the product of your art the greatest good?' 'How can it be otherwise, Socrates,' he will presumably say, 'seeing that it is health? What greater good can a man possess than health?' Suppose next that the trainer were to say: 'I [b] should be surprised, Socrates, if Gorgias could demonstrate to you that a greater good comes from his art than does from mine', I should say to him, as I did to the doctor: 'And you, my good man, who are you and what is your job?' 'I am a trainer,' he would say, 'and my job is to make men physically beautiful and strong.' After the trainer the man of business c would have his say, filled, I suppose, with a fine contempt for them all: 'Do you really think, Socrates, that a greater good than wealth is to be found either with Gorgias or with anyone else?' 'What?' we should say to him, 'are you the man who produces wealth?' 'Yes.' 'In what capacity?' 'As a man of business.' 'Well,' we should say, 'do you think that wealth is the greatest good for mankind?' 'Of course.' 'And yet', we should go on, 'here is Gorgias who maintains that the art which he possesses is productive of a greater good than yours.' Obviously he would ask next: 'What is this good? Let Gorgias answer.'

d So then, Gorgias, imagine that you are being asked this question by these men as well as by me, and tell us what it is that you declare to be the greatest human good that you claim to be able to produce.

GORGIAS: I mean, Socrates, what is in truth the greatest good, which confers on everyone who possesses it not only freedom for himself but also the power of ruling his fellow-citizens.

SOCRATES: What do you mean by that?

e GORGIAS: I mean the ability to convince by means of speech a jury in a court of justice, members of the Council in their Chamber, those attending a meeting of the Assembly, and any other gathering of citizens whatever it may be.[14] By the exercise of this ability you will have the doctor as your slave, the trainer as your slave, and that businessman of yours will turn out to be making money not for himself but for another – for you, in fact, who have the ability to speak and to convince the masses.

453 SOCRATES: Now, Gorgias, I think that you have defined with great precision what you take the art of oratory to be, and, if I understand you correctly, you are saying that oratory is a maker of conviction,[15] and that this is the sum and substance

of its whole activity. Or have you some further power to ascribe to oratory beyond that of producing conviction in the souls of its hearers?

GORGIAS: No, Socrates; the definition which you have given seems to be quite adequate; that sums up oratory.

SOCRATES: Listen then, Gorgias. If ever anyone made it his object in discussion to know exactly what the discussion is about, I am quite sure – and you may be sure too – that I am such a man, and I believe that I should be right in saying that you are another. b

GORGIAS: What follows from that, Socrates?

SOCRATES: I'll tell you. This conviction produced by oratory that you speak of – I really have no clear knowledge what it is or what it is conviction about. I won't say that I haven't a suspicion of your meaning on both points, but that won't prevent me from asking you what you believe to be the nature of the conviction produced by oratory and the subject of that conviction. So why, if I have this suspicion, do I ask *you* instead of answering the question myself? Not out of consideration for you but so that it will progress the argument in such a way as to put what we are discussing in the clearest possible light. See if you agree that my questions are fair if you look at the matter like this. Suppose I were asking you what sort of painter Zeuxis[16] is, and you replied that he is a painter of pictures; wouldn't I be justified in asking you what sort of pictures he paints and where? c

GORGIAS: Certainly.

SOCRATES: Because there are other painters who paint many other kinds of picture? d

GORGIAS: Yes.

SOCRATES: But if Zeuxis were the only picture painter your answer would have been right?

GORGIAS: Of course.

SOCRATES: Well, now take oratory. Do you think that oratory is the only art that creates conviction or do other arts create it as well? I mean something like this: does whoever teaches a subject create conviction or not?

GORGIAS: Of course he does, Socrates; unquestionably.

e SOCRATES: Again, if we take the other arts mentioned just now, do not arithmetic and the arithmetician teach us all that concerns number?

GORGIAS: Certainly.

SOCRATES: And therefore also create conviction?

GORGIAS: Yes.

SOCRATES: Then arithmetic as well as oratory produces conviction?

GORGIAS: It would seem so.

SOCRATES: And if someone asks us what sort of conviction 454 and conviction about what, we shall of course tell him that it is conviction of the kind created by teaching about odd and even and their magnitude. And similarly with all the other arts we mentioned just now; we shall be able to show, shan't we, not only that they produce conviction but also the nature and subject of that conviction?

GORGIAS: Yes.

SOCRATES: Then oratory is not the only creator of conviction.

GORGIAS: True.

SOCRATES: Then, since other arts besides oratory discharge this function, we shall be justified in asking again, as we did about the painter, the nature and subject of the conviction which is the peculiar province of the art of oratory. Or don't b you think it right to repeat the question?

GORGIAS: Yes, I do.

SOCRATES: Answer then, Gorgias, since you share my opinion.

GORGIAS: Oratory serves, Socrates, to produce the kind of conviction needed in courts of law and other large masses of people, as I was saying just now, and the subject of this kind of conviction is right and wrong.[17]

SOCRATES: That is just what I suspected you meant, Gorgias. But don't be surprised if a little later on I repeat this procedure c and ask additional questions when the answer seems to be already clear. This, as I say, is not aimed at you personally; it is simply to help the discussion to progress towards its end in a logical sequence and to prevent us from getting into the habit of snatching prematurely at one another's statements because we have a vague suspicion what they are likely to be, instead of allowing you to develop your argument in your own way from the agreed foundations.

GORGIAS: A thoroughly sound method, Socrates.

Note that Gorgias has himself introduced, unforced by Socrates, two points which become important in the subsequent dialogue: his art is about power (452e1) and is concerned with right and wrong (454b7). Socrates makes clear (b9) that these are points to which he will return.

A[4] 454c7–457c3

Socrates suggests another distinction, agreed to by Gorgias, between conviction based on knowledge, which must be true (you can't have false knowledge) and conviction based on belief, which can be either true or false. Gorgias' placing of oratory on the side of belief without knowledge (at 454e8) might seem to us an unnecessary concession at this stage of the argument – and note that Socrates does not, ostensibly, 'force' the choice on him at e5 ff.; why can't oratory concern itself with knowledge and what is true? Moreover, we might be equally unconvinced by the élitist assumption they both appear to share, that addressing a mass audience precludes serious 'teaching' (455a5–7). But Gorgias' choice here does have major consequences for the subsequent argument (as Socrates later points out – see below section A[6]).

Socrates then broadens the discussion into the area of practical politics (and foreshadows his attack on Athenian democracy later in the dialogue): when the Athenian Assembly makes decisions about expert matters, such as equipping harbours, building walls or appointing generals, it is orators and not the professionals, Gorgias boasts, who get their way. At the end of this section of the argument (456c7 ff.), however, Gorgias goes on to introduce a limitation on the orator's power, that he ought not to make bad use of it, and cannot be held responsible if pupils do so. Socrates will return shortly to this proviso and its fatal consequences for Gorgias' position (see A[6] below).

SOCRATES: Now let us consider this point. You would agree that there is such a thing as 'knowing'?

GORGIAS: Certainly.

SOCRATES: And such as thing as 'believing'?

d GORGIAS: Yes.

SOCRATES: Well, do you think that knowing and believing are the same, or is there a difference between knowledge and belief?

GORGIAS: I should say that there is a difference.

SOCRATES: Quite right; and you can prove it like this. If you were asked if there is true and false belief, you would say that there is, no doubt.

GORGIAS: Yes.

SOCRATES: Well then, is there true and false knowledge?

GORGIAS: Certainly not.

SOCRATES: Then knowledge and belief are clearly not the same thing.

GORGIAS: True.

e SOCRATES: Yet those who have been persuaded into believing something may just as properly be called convinced as those who have learned it?

GORGIAS: Yes.

SOCRATES: May we then establish that there are two kinds of conviction, one which gives knowledge and one which gives belief without knowledge?

GORGIAS: Certainly.

SOCRATES: Now which kind of conviction does oratory produce about right and wrong in courts of law and with other large masses: the kind which engenders knowledge or the kind which engenders belief without knowledge?

GORGIAS: The kind which engenders belief, obviously.

SOCRATES: Oratory, then, as it seems, produces conviction 455 about right and wrong which is a matter of persuasion and belief, not the result of teaching and learning?

GORGIAS: Yes.

SOCRATES: And the orator does not teach juries and other large masses about right and wrong – he merely persuades them; he could hardly teach so large a mass of people matters of such importance in a short time.[18]

GORGIAS: Of course he couldn't.

SOCRATES: Come now, let us see what our statements about b oratory actually amount to; I don't mind admitting that for my own part I still haven't a clear idea what I think about it. Whenever the citizens hold a meeting to appoint medical officers[19] or shipbuilders or any other professional worker, surely it won't be the orator who advises them then? Obviously in every such election they have to choose the most expert; if it is a question of building walls or equipping harbours or dockyards, it is architects whose opinion will be asked; if again it is the appointment of generals or the order of battle against an enemy or the capture of strongholds that is being debated, men of experience in war will be called on for advice, not orators. What is your opinion about this, c Gorgias? You claim to be an orator yourself and capable of producing orators; so it makes sense to learn from you about your own art. And in doing so I have your interests at heart as well, believe me. It may be that there is someone present now who wishes to be your pupil; in fact I notice that there are some, in fact quite a few, but they are perhaps shy of putting questions to you. Imagine then that they as well as I d are saying to you: 'What advantage shall we gain, Gorgias, if we associate with you? On what subjects shall we be able to advise the city? Simply about right and wrong, or about the other subjects too which Socrates has mentioned?' Try to give them an answer.

GORGIAS: Well, I will try, Socrates, to reveal to you clearly the whole power of oratory; your own remarks make an admirable introduction. You know of course that Athens owes its dockyards and walls and the equipping of harbours e partly to the advice of Themistocles[20] and partly to that of Pericles, but not to that of the professional builders.

SOCRATES: That is what we are told about Themistocles, Gorgias. As for Pericles, I heard him myself when he was proposing the building of the Middle Wall.[21]

456 GORGIAS: And you can see that when there is a choice to be made of the kind that you spoke of just now it is the orators who give advice and get their proposals adopted.

SOCRATES: I do see it, and it fills me with amazement, Gorgias. That is why I have been asking you all this time what the power of oratory consists in. When I look at it like this its greatness seems practically supernatural.

GORGIAS: You might well be amazed, Socrates, if you knew the whole truth and realized that oratory embraces and controls almost all other spheres of human activity. I can give you a b striking proof of this. It has often happened that I have gone with my brother and other doctors to visit some sick person who refused to drink his medicine or to submit to surgery or cautery, and when the doctors could not persuade him I have succeeded, simply by my use of the art of oratory. I tell you that, if in any city you care to name, an orator and a doctor had to compete before the Assembly or in any other gathering for the appointment of a medical officer, the man who could c speak would be appointed if he wanted the post, and the doctor would end up nowhere. Similarly, if he had to compete with any other professional worker the orator could get himself appointed against any opposition; there is no subject on which he could not speak before a popular audience more persuasively than any professional of whatever kind. Such is the nature and power of the art of oratory, Socrates, but it should be used as with any other competitive skill. Just d because a man has acquired such skills in boxing or all-in wrestling or armed combat that he can beat anyone, friend or foe, that is no reason why he should employ it against all men indiscriminately and strike and wound and kill his friends. Nor yet, by Zeus, if a course at the training school has put a man in a good condition and made him a boxer, and he then strikes his father or mother or some relation or friend, that is e no reason for detesting and banishing trainers and those who teach the use of weapons; for they passed on these skills intending that they should be put to a good use against the country's enemies and against wrongdoers, defensively, not 457 aggressively, and if their pupils on the contrary make bad use of their strength and skill it does not follow that the teachers are criminal or the art which they teach culpable and wicked; the fault rests with those who do not make a proper use of it. The same argument holds good about oratory. The orator is able to speak on any subject against any opposition so as to be more persuasive in front of the masses – in short – on any b topic he chooses, but the fact that he possesses the power to deprive doctors and other professionals of their reputation does not justify him in doing so; but he must use his oratory rightly as with any other competitive skill. I think that if a man who has acquired oratorical skill then uses the power which his art confers to do wrong, that is no reason to detest his teacher and banish him from the city. His instruction was given to be employed for good ends, whereas the pupil is c using it in the opposite way; so it is right to hate and banish and kill the one who does not use his skill rightly, but not his teacher.

Note how, right from the beginning of the dialogue, Socrates' suggestions of a variety of distinctions in classification of arts force Gorgias to narrow down his definition of oratory and say precisely what its functions and scope are, as opposed to those of other arts. Gorgias' choices at every turn paint a portrait of a man who is not intellectually very acute; he believes that he is being given an opportunity to show off the fine qualities of his art; but by making such extravagant claims for his art and then disclaiming responsibility for its misuse, in reality he is, from Socrates' point of view, digging his own grave.

A[5] 457c4–458e2

There is a short interlude in the discussion. Plato often inserts such pauses in his dialogues to indicate that the argument has reached a provisional resting-point and to allow Socrates and the other participants to reflect for a moment on the conduct (as opposed to the content) of the discussion. Here Socrates enlarges on a matter he has alluded to at intervals throughout the discussion so far (e.g. 454c1 ff.) – the importance of arguing not in order to score points off an opponent (a practice known as eristic*) but co-operatively, for the sake of mutual enlightenment. He holds out to Gorgias the possibility of ending the discussion, and Gorgias seems initially inclined to accept, but the other participants (and bystanders, 458c3) are anxious that it should continue.*

SOCRATES: I suppose, Gorgias, that like me you have had experience of many arguments, and have observed how difficult the parties find it to define exactly the subject which they have taken in hand and to come away from their discussion d mutually enlightened; what usually happens is that, as soon as they disagree and one declares the other to be mistaken or obscure in what he says, they lose their tempers and accuse one another of speaking from motives of personal spite[22] and in an endeavour to score a victory rather than to investigate the question at issue; and sometimes they part on the worst possible terms, after such an exchange of abuse that the bystanders feel annoyed on their own account that they ever thought it worth their while to listen to such people. Now, e why do I say this? It is because what you are saying now does not appear to me quite consistent or in harmony with what you said at first about oratory, and I am afraid to examine you further in case you suppose that I am in competition, not in order to clarify the issue but to defeat you. And so, if you are the same sort of person as myself, I will willingly go on 458 questioning you; otherwise I will stop. And what sort of man am I? I am one of those people who are glad to have their own mistakes pointed out and glad to point out the mistakes of others, but who would just as soon have the first experience as the second; in fact I consider being refuted a greater good, inasmuch as it is better to be relieved of a very bad evil oneself than to relieve another. In my opinion no worse evil can befall a man than to have a false belief about the subjects which we are now discussing. So if you are of the b same mind, let us go on with the conversation; but if you think that we ought to abandon it let us drop it at once and bring the argument to an end.

GORGIAS: Personally, Socrates, I would claim to be just the sort of person you have indicated, but perhaps we ought to consider the rest of the company. Before your arrival I had already given them a long display, and it may perhaps prolong things too much to go on with this argument. We ought to consult their wishes as well as our own; it may be that we are keeping some of them when they have other things to do. c

CHAEREPHON: You can judge for yourselves by the noise they are making, Gorgias and Socrates, that everybody is anxious to hear whatever you may have to say. For my part, I hope that I should never be so busy as to have to abandon for something more important a discussion so interesting as this and so ably conducted.

CALLICLES: By the gods, Chaerephon, I too have been present at many discussions, but I don't believe that any has ever given me so much pleasure as this. If you like to go on talking all day, you are doing me a favour. d

SOCRATES: Well, there is no objection on my side, Callicles, if Gorgias is willing.

GORGIAS: It would be a disgrace[23] for me not to be willing, Socrates, after my spontaneous offer to reply to any question. So, if our friends here approve, go on with the conversation and ask me anything you like. e

Socrates' politeness has an ironic edge; deference to Gorgias' intellectual eminence contrasts with the ease with which Socrates is leading the sophist into an illogical position (and perhaps we can see Gorgias' own dim awareness of the consequences for his personal prestige at 458d7). Is Socrates being entirely sincere in emphasizing the non-adversarial nature of his habitual conduct of such discussions? Does he protest too much here? Concern for appropriate conduct of the discussion is highly relevant, however, in view of the much more abrasive exchanges with other participants which are to come.

A[6] 458e3–461b2

In this final section of the dialogue with Gorgias, Socrates draws out the fatal consequences of the sophist's earlier admissions. When Gorgias agreed that the orator would be more persuasive before a mass audience than the expert (455a7 ff.), this amounts, Socrates suggests, to saying that 'an ignorant person is more convincing than the expert before an equally ignorant audience' (459b3–5). Socrates then moves on from other areas of expertise to questions of value, which Gorgias had said (454b7) were the particular province of the orator: is the orator equally ignorant about right and wrong, or is knowledge of these a prior condition of the apprentice orator coming to Gorgias for instruction? Gorgias' reply that he will teach such matters 'if [the pupil] happens not to know them' (460a3–4), leads Socrates on to a sequence of argument (460b2–c6) that argues by analogy with other arts that knowledge of a subject gives the expert the character which the knowledge confers; so knowledge of right makes a man righteous, and, Socrates maintains, the righteous man will never wish to do wrong. So an oratorical pupil, if rightly taught, cannot make a wrong use of his art (as Gorgias has suggested at 456d1 ff.).

SOCRATES: Listen, then, to the point that surprises me in what you said, Gorgias; it may be that you are right and I don't understand you properly. You say that you can make an orator of anyone who wishes to learn from you?

GORGIAS: Yes.

SOCRATES: And consequently in all matters he will be able to get his way before a mass of people not by teaching but by convincing?

459 GORGIAS: Certainly.

SOCRATES: You said just now that even on matters of health the orator will be more convincing than the doctor.

GORGIAS: Before a mass audience – yes, I did.

SOCRATES: A mass audience means an ignorant audience,

doesn't it? He won't be more convincing than the doctor before experts, I presume.

GORGIAS: True.

SOCRATES: Now, if he is more convincing than the doctor then does he turn out to be more convincing than the expert?

GORGIAS: Naturally.

SOCRATES: Not being a doctor, of course? b

GORGIAS: Of course.

SOCRATES: And the non-doctor, presumably, is ignorant of what the doctor knows?

GORGIAS: Obviously.

SOCRATES: So when the orator is more convincing than the doctor, what happens is that an ignorant person is more convincing than the expert before an equally ignorant audience. Is this what happens?

GORGIAS: This is what happens in that case, no doubt.

SOCRATES: And the same will be true of the orator and oratory in relation to all other arts. The orator need have no knowledge of the truth about things; it is enough for him to have discovered a knack of persuading the ignorant that he seems to know more than the experts. c

GORGIAS: And isn't it a great comfort, Socrates, never to be beaten by specialists in all the other arts without going to the trouble of acquiring more than this single one?

SOCRATES: We will discuss in a moment, if it turns out to be relevant, whether the orator does or does not lose to the others; but first of all let us consider how he stands with regard to right and wrong, honour and dishonour, good and d bad. Is he in the same position here as he is about health and the objects of the other arts, quite ignorant of the actual nature of good and bad or honour and dishonour or right and wrong, but contriving a power of persuasion which enables him, in spite of his ignorance, to appear to the ignorant wiser than those who know? Or must he have prior e knowledge and understanding of all these matters before he comes to you to be taught oratory? And if not – for it is not your business, as a teacher of oratory, to teach your pupil about these things – will you then, if he comes to you ignorant of them, enable him to acquire a popular reputation for knowledge and goodness when in fact he possesses neither? Or will you be quite unable to teach him oratory at all unless he knows the truth about these things beforehand? What are

460 we to think about all this, Gorgias? Do, by Zeus, keep the promise you made a short time ago and reveal to us what the power of oratory is.

GORGIAS: I suppose, Socrates, that a pupil will also learn these things from me, if he happens not to know them.

SOCRATES: Stop there; that is an excellent answer. If you are to make a man an orator, he must either know right and wrong *before* he comes to you or learn them from you *after* becoming your pupil.

b GORGIAS: Certainly.

SOCRATES: Well now, a man who has learnt carpentry is a carpenter, isn't he?

GORGIAS: Yes.

SOCRATES: And a man who has learnt music a musician?

GORGIAS: Yes.

SOCRATES: And a man who has learnt medicine a doctor, and so on. In fact a man who has learnt any subject possesses the character which knowledge of that subject confers.

GORGIAS: Of course.

SOCRATES: Then by the same reckoning a man who has learnt about right will be righteous?

GORGIAS: Unquestionably.

SOCRATES: And a righteous man performs right actions, I presume.

GORGIAS: Yes.

c SOCRATES: Then the orator will of necessity be a righteous man and a righteous man will want to perform right actions.

GORGIAS: Apparently.

SOCRATES: Then the righteous man will never want to do wrong.

GORGIAS: Never.

SOCRATES: And according to the argument, the orator must be righteous.

GORGIAS: Yes.

SOCRATES: Then the orator will never wish to do wrong.

GORGIAS: Apparently not.

SOCRATES: Now do you remember that you said a short time ago[24] that if a boxer makes a wrong use of his skill and does wrong, that is no reason for blaming his trainers and sending them into exile, and similarly if an orator employs his oratory wrongly we ought not to blame or banish his teacher, but the man who actually does wrong and uses his art amiss. You did say that didn't you? d

GORGIAS: I did.

SOCRATES: But now it appears, doesn't it, that this same orator would never have done wrong? e

GORGIAS: It seems so.

SOCRATES: Moreover, at the beginning of our discussion, Gorgias, it was stated that oratory was concerned with speech, not speech about odd and even but speech about right and wrong. Do you remember?

GORGIAS: Yes.

SOCRATES: Now, when you were saying that, I assumed that oratory could never be a bad thing because it is always talking about right. But when shortly afterwards, you were saying that an orator might make a wrong use of oratory I was surprised at the inconsistency, and it was then that I remarked that if you were like me in counting it a gain to have your mistakes pointed out, it would be worthwhile going on with the conversation, but if not, we had better let it drop. You see for yourself that further consideration has led to our agreeing that it is impossible for the orator to make a wrong use of his oratory and to want to do wrong. What are we to make of this? By the dog,[25] Gorgias, it will need more than a short discussion if we are to get to the bottom of it to our satisfaction. 461 b

In this culmination of the dialogue with Gorgias there is the sense that Socrates' moves in the discussion are designed to trap a weak opponent, render him 'dialectically ambushed' (Beversluis 2000, p. 314), rather than to engender real conviction in the reader at

this stage of the argument. A number of objections come to mind: earlier on we saw that Gorgias perhaps too hastily gave up claims to knowledge – the orator may not be an expert in a particular art like builders or generals, but, as a politician in the Assembly (see 455b1 ff.), he may well have a worthwhile judgement about how an art should be applied, and when, e.g. how fortifications should be deployed, when war should be declared – matters which are not the province of any particular technical expert, but which may still be called knowledge.

Socrates' particular assumptions about the implications of expert knowledge are also at work in the sequence at 460b1 ff.: he argues that just as someone who has learned about music is a musician, so someone who has learned about right will be righteous, and therefore will not want to do wrong (and this contradicts what Gorgias has conceded at 456d1 ff.). Socrates seems to be assuming that knowledge of what is right automatically *entails the desire to perform right actions: 'the righteous man will never want to do wrong' (460c3). This startling and, to the modern mind, improbable conclusion, that morality can be acquired as a kind of knowledge similar to any other, is explored further in the dialogue with Polus (B[2] below).*

Socrates may well be guilty of a particular sleight of hand in this opening dialogue, as Polus asserts (B[1] below), but his questions do reveal Gorgias' genuine confusion or even social embarrassment at having to concede the apparent logical weaknesses in his position. Also, in introducing Socrates' beliefs on key themes such as knowledge, power and the orator's implied ignorance of what is right and wrong, Plato foreshadows the subsequent development of the dialogue.

B: DIALOGUE WITH POLUS 461b3–481b5

B[1] 461b3–466a3

Polus sharply and characteristically bursts in at this point (as he did unsuccessfully right at the beginning, above A[1]). Accusing Socrates of arguing personally against Gorgias simply to win (a charge which Socrates took some trouble to anticipate at 454b–c), Polus accurately fixes on the threat of suffering from aischune *(shame, loss of face) which led Gorgias into inconsistency by making him unwilling to admit that orators might not know about right and wrong. When invited to take Gorgias' place, Polus asks Socrates what sort of art he thinks oratory to be, and receives the answer that in Socrates' view it is not an art at all, but a 'knack'* (empeiria = *'something developed by experience') as opposed to a* techne, *an art or craft which can give a rational account of its procedures and which can therefore be taught. The former, which may look genuine to the uninitiated, is guided by no rational theory, but operates by a sort of 'rule of thumb' and is concerned merely to satisfy desires and give gratification and pleasure. Once again, we might dispute the division (are cookery and beauty-culture not in their own ways* 'arts'? *– experts in these fields would certainly argue so!), but Polus does not do so here. Socrates proceeds to develop a classificatory division (he has already attempted an informal classification with Gorgias in A [1 and 2]) in which a number of genuine arts have their pseudo-art counterparts; they are also divided as to whether they relate to the body or the soul. Socrates' classification at 464b2 ff. might be formalized like this:*

	Soul		Body	
Genuine art	Legislation	Justice	Training	Medicine
Spurious art	Sophistry	Oratory	Beauty-culture	Cookery

The tone of the discussion, under Socrates' (here transparent) veneer of ironic politeness, becomes more abrasive and confrontational.

POLUS: What, Socrates? Can you really believe what you are saying about oratory? Or do you imagine – just because Gorgias was ashamed not to concede to you that the orator must know what is right and fine and good, and asserted that if a pupil came to him ignorant of these things he would teach him himself. And then this admission on his part made the
c argument appear inconsistent, which is just the sort of thing you love, deliberately entrapping people in such questions – who do you imagine[26] is going to admit that he doesn't know himself and can't teach others the nature of right? It is very ill-bred to lead the discussion in such a direction.

SOCRATES: Polus, my very good friend, it is at just such moments as this that we need the services of friends and sons, so that when we older folk trip up in word or deed, you of the younger generation may be there to set us on our feet
d again. And so now, if Gorgias and I trip up in our argument, come and set us right – you are perfectly justified in doing that. And if you think that we are mistaken in any of our conclusions, I'm perfectly willing to take back anything you like, but on one condition.

POLUS: What is that?

SOCRATES: That you keep in check the long speeches which you embarked on at the beginning of our conversation.[27]

POLUS: What? Am I not allowed to say as much as I choose?

e SOCRATES: It would certainly be hard luck, my good friend, if on arriving in Athens, which allows freedom of speech above all other cities in Greece, you found that you alone were denied that privilege. But, just look at the other side, think what hard luck it will be for me if, when you are making a long speech and refusing to answer the questions put to you, 462 I am not to be allowed to go away and get out of hearing. No – if you care at all about the present argument and want to set it on the right lines, accept my offer to take back any step in it you like, and by asking and answering questions in turn, like Gorgias and myself, examine and be examined alternately. You would claim, I suppose, that you know as much as Gorgias?

POLUS: I would indeed.

SOCRATES: In that case, don't you, like Gorgias, invite people to put any question to you at any time, relying on your ability to answer?

POLUS: Certainly.

SOCRATES: Well, would you rather ask or answer at the present b moment? Make your choice.

POLUS: I will; *you* answer me, Socrates. Since you think Gorgias confused about the nature of oratory, you tell me what you take oratory to be.

SOCRATES: Are you asking me what sort of art I take it to be?

POLUS: Yes, indeed.

SOCRATES: No art at all, Polus, if I'm to tell you the truth.

POLUS: What do you think it is then?

SOCRATES: A thing which you say in a treatise I read lately[28] is the creator of art. c

POLUS: What do you mean?

SOCRATES: I should call it a sort of knack gained by experience.[29]

POLUS: You think oratory is a sort of knack?

SOCRATES: Subject to your correction, I do.

POLUS: A knack of doing what?

SOCRATES: Producing a kind of gratification and pleasure.

POLUS: In that case, if it is able to give people gratification, don't you consider it a fine thing?

SOCRATES: What, Polus? Do you feel so adequately informed

d already of my views on the nature of oratory that you pass on to the next question – whether I consider it a fine thing?

POLUS: Didn't you tell me that you consider it a sort of knack?

SOCRATES: You set a high value on gratification; will you gratify me in a small matter?

POLUS: By all means.

SOCRATES: Just ask me, will you, what sort of art I take cookery to be.

POLUS: All right, I'm asking you: what sort of art is cookery?

SOCRATES: It isn't an art at all, Polus. Now say, 'What is it then?'

POLUS: All right, I say it.[30]

SOCRATES: A kind of knack gained by experience, I should say.

POLUS: A knack of doing what? Tell me.

e SOCRATES: Producing gratification and pleasure, Polus.

POLUS: Then are oratory and cookery the same thing?

SOCRATES: Certainly not, but they are branches of the same occupation.

POLUS: What occupation do you mean?

SOCRATES: I'm afraid that the truth may sound rather blunt, and I wouldn't like Gorgias to think that I am making fun of 463 his profession. Whether this is the sort of oratory that he practises, I don't know; our argument just now shed no light on his own views on the subject.[31] But what I call oratory is a branch of something which certainly isn't a fine or honourable pursuit.

GORGIAS: What do you mean, Socrates? Speak out and don't be afraid of hurting my feelings.

SOCRATES: Well, Gorgias, oratory seems to me to be a pursuit which has nothing to do with art, but which requires a shrewd and bold spirit naturally clever at dealing with people. The b generic name which I should give it is pandering;[32] it has many subdivisions, one of which is cookery, an occupation which masquerades as an art but by my argument is no more than a knack acquired by routine. Under this heading I would add oratory and beauty-culture and sophistry – making four distinct branches corresponding to four distinct fields of activity. If Polus likes to question me about this he is welcome to do so; it doesn't seem to have struck him that I have not yet explained where I place oratory among the subdivisions of pandering. He goes on to ask the further question, whether I don't think oratory an honourable pursuit; but I won't say whether I think oratory honourable or shameful before I have explained what it really is – that would not be right. However, if you care to ask me, Polus, where oratory stands among the subdivisions of pandering, ask away.[33] c

POLUS: Very well then; what branch of pandering is oratory?

SOCRATES: I'm not sure that you will understand the answer. In my view oratory is a semblance of a branch of the art of politics. d

POLUS: And then what? Do you call it honourable or dishonourable?

SOCRATES: Dishonourable undoubtedly, if you insist on an answer, for I would call anything that is bad dishonourable. But this is to assume that you have already grasped my meaning.

GORGIAS: By Zeus, Socrates, I don't understand your meaning either.

SOCRATES: Of course you don't, Gorgias; I haven't yet made it plain. But Polus here has all the impatience of youth.[34] e

GORGIAS: Never mind him; tell *me* what you mean when you call oratory a semblance of a branch of the art of politics.

SOCRATES: Well, I'll try to explain my view of the nature of oratory; if I'm wrong, Polus here will correct me. Presumably you admit the existence of body and soul? 464

GORGIAS: Of course.

SOCRATES: And you would agree that there is a state of health corresponding to each of these?

GORGIAS: Yes.

SOCRATES: And also such a thing as an unreal appearance of health? For example, many people appear to enjoy health in whom nobody but a doctor or trainer could detect the reverse.

GORGIAS: True.

SOCRATES: I maintain that there is a condition of soul as well as body[35] which gives the appearance of health without the reality.

b GORGIAS: Quite right.

SOCRATES: Now, I'll put my meaning in a clearer light, if I can. I maintain that these two, body and soul, have two arts corresponding to them; that which deals with the soul I call the political art, but though the subject of physical welfare constitutes a unity, I cannot offhand find a single name for the art which deals with the body, and which has two branches, training and medicine. In the art of politics what corresponds to training is called legislation and what corresponds to medicine the administration of justice. The members of each of these pairs, training and medicine, legislation and justice, c have something in common, because they are concerned with the same object, but they are different from one another none the less. We have then these four arts, constantly concerned with the highest welfare of body and soul respectively; and the pseudo-art of the pander, being instinctively aware of this division of function though it has no accurate knowledge, divides itself also into four branches, and putting on the guise d of each of the genuine arts, pretends to be the art which it is impersonating.

The difference is that pandering pays no regard to the best interests of its object, but catches fools with the bait of ephemeral pleasure and tricks them into holding it in the highest esteem. Thus, cookery puts on the mask of medicine and pretends to know what foods are best for the body, and, if a doctor or a cook had to compete before an audience of children or of men with no more sense than children, with the job of deciding which of them is the better judge of e wholesome and unwholesome foodstuffs, the doctor would unquestionably die of hunger.[36] Now I call this sort of thing 465 pandering and I declare that it is dishonourable – I'm addressing you now, Polus – because it makes pleasure its aim instead of good, and I maintain that it is merely a knack and not an art because it has no rational understanding of the nature of the various things it applies to or the person to whom it applies, so that it can't explain anything. I refuse to give the title of art to anything irrational, and if you dispute any of this I am ready to justify my position.

Cookery then, as I say, is the form of pandering which is disguised as medicine, and in the same way physical training has its counterfeit in beauty-culture, a mischievous, swindling, base, servile trade, which creates an illusion by the use of artificial adjuncts and make-up and depilatories and costume, and makes people assume a borrowed beauty to the neglect of the true beauty which is the product of training. In short, I will put the matter in the form of a geometrical proportion – perhaps now you will be able to follow me – and say that as beauty-culture is to physical training so is sophistry to legislation and that as cookery is to medicine so is oratory to justice.[37] There is, I repeat, an essential difference between sophists and orators,[38] but because they border on one another they are liable to be confused in the popular mind as occupying common ground and being engaged in the same pursuit; in fact sophists and orators no more know what to make of themselves than the world at large knows what to make of them. The same confusion would occur with cookery and medicine if the body were left to its own devices instead of being controlled by the soul, which distinguishes the two from its superior viewpoint; if the body had to draw this distinction with no criterion but its own sensations of pleasure, the saying of Anaxagoras – with which you are so well acquainted, my dear Polus – would apply far and wide. 'All things together' would be all mixed up,[39] and there would be no boundaries between the provinces of medicine and health and cookery.

Now, you have heard my view of the nature of oratory; it is to the soul what cookery is to the body. Perhaps it may seem strange that after forbidding you to make a long speech I should have spun out my own to such a length. My excuse is that when I spoke more briefly you didn't understand; you couldn't make anything of the answer I gave you and begged for an explanation. If I in my turn find myself in difficulties about your answers, you too develop them more fully, otherwise let me – that's only right. And now if you have any reply to this, fire away.

b c d e 466

B[2] 466a4–468e5

This section takes up the second major theme of the dialogue as a whole, already introduced by Gorgias in the first section (A [3 and 4] above): the question of political power. Without conceding that Socrates' long speech classifying real and pseudo-arts (B[1] above), has convinced him, Polus argues – what seems to him self-evident – that orators at least have power. *Socrates' opposing argument has two stages:*

1. He makes a distinction between doing what seems best (what one decides to do) and what one wants. Orators and tyrants do what seems best to them but they don't do what they (really) want, because they are ignorant of what is in their best interests.

2. This paradoxical division between 'what seems best' and 'what one wants' is explained by a distinction between means and ends: when we act towards a given end, we do not want the means to an end, for example drinking unpleasant medicine, but the good end to which the unpleasant means is directed, i.e. health. The object of what individuals want (as opposed to what seems best to them) is always good (i.e. brings genuine advantage to the doer – the ancient Greeks did not on the whole recognize altruistic or disinterested motivation for moral action). The only real power is that which aims at the good. Since orators and tyrants are ignorant, they are invariably misled about their real interests (the ends of their actions), and so, when doing evil deeds, for example, confiscation of others' property and banishment, which 'seems best to them', they do not do what is good for themselves (i.e. gaining genuine advantage) and so do not have real power. Doing what one thinks best (what one decides) is irrational – satisfaction of desires for pleasure – while doing what one wants is rational, that is, knowing what benefits one's actions bring.

Of course, this leaves open the question whether (conventionally) evil deeds might actually be good for you (to your advantage), which becomes a major theme later in the dialogue. But here Socrates' insistence that one only really wants *what is good is based on Plato's intellectualist view of knowledge – to* know *the good necessarily entails* doing *it and doing evil implies being mistaken about one's real interests (see A[6] above).*

The comparison of orators with tyrants in their exercise of power (made by Polus at 466b11) becomes in the course of the discussion a close identification of the two groups and an important point in the dialogue as a whole; since effective oratory in the ancient world was the key to political power, the move from oratory to tyranny is a natural one for Plato, and allows Socrates to confront what he sees as the misguided exercise of power in its extreme form.

POLUS: So, what are you saying? You think that oratory is pandering?

SOCRATES: I said that it was a branch of pandering. Your memory is very bad for someone so young, Polus. What will happen to you by and by?

POLUS: And do you think that good orators are meanly thought of in a state, and regarded as panders?

SOCRATES: Is this a question or the beginning of a speech? b

POLUS: It's a question I'm asking.

SOCRATES: In my opinion they are not thought of[40] at all.

POLUS: Not thought of? Have they not very great power in the city?

SOCRATES: If by power you mean something that is good for its possessor, no.

POLUS: That is what I do mean.

SOCRATES: Then in that case I consider orators the least powerful people in the city.

POLUS: What? Can they not kill whoever they want to, like tyrants,[41] and confiscate possessions and banish from the city c anyone they please?

SOCRATES: By the dog, Polus, whenever you open your mouth I'm in doubt whether you are expressing your own opinion or asking me a question.

POLUS: I'm asking you a question.

SOCRATES: In that case you are asking me two questions at once, my friend.

POLUS: Two questions? What do you mean?

SOCRATES: Didn't you say just now that orators, like tyrants,
d can kill whoever they want to and confiscate possessions and banish from the city anyone they please?

POLUS: Yes.

SOCRATES: Well, I maintain that there are two questions here, and I will answer them both. In my view, Polus, as I have already said, orators and tyrants are the least powerful persons in a city. They do practically nothing that they want
e to, only what they think best.

POLUS: Well, isn't that to have great power?

SOCRATES: According to Polus, no.

POLUS: According to me? But I say it is.

SOCRATES: By the – ;[42] no, you don't. You said that great power was good for its possessor.

POLUS: Yes I do say that.

SOCRATES: Well, do you think it good when a man devoid of wisdom does what seems best to him? Do you call that great power?

POLUS: No.

SOCRATES: Then won't you prove me wrong, and show that
467 orators are men of wisdom, and oratory an art and not mere pandering? Otherwise orators who do what they please in a city, and tyrants too, for that matter, will have acquired nothing good from it, since according to you power is a good thing, but doing what one pleases without wisdom is by your own admission a bad thing. You do admit that, don't you?

POLUS: Yes.

SOCRATES: Then unless Polus can show Socrates that he was wrong and prove that oratory and tyrants do what they really want, how can they be said to enjoy great power in a state?

b POLUS: This fellow –

SOCRATES: Says that they don't do what they really want. So prove me wrong.

POLUS: Didn't you admit just now that they do what seems best to them?

SOCRATES: Certainly; I don't retract it.

POLUS: Then don't they do what they want?
SOCRATES: No.
POLUS: Although they do what seems right to them?
SOCRATES: Yes.
POLUS: What you say is monstrous and outrageous, Socrates.
SOCRATES: Don't use hard words, my peerless Polus, if I may address you for once in your own alliterative style.[43] Prove my mistake by your questions, if you still have any to ask, or else let us change parts, and you do the answering. c
POLUS: Very well, I don't mind answering, in order to get at your meaning.
SOCRATES: Do you think that when people do something, at any time, they want their act itself or the object of their act? Take, for example, patients who drink medicine on doctor's orders. Do you think that they want the act of drinking the medicine with its attendant pain or the object of the act, that is, health?
POLUS: Health, obviously.
SOCRATES: Similarly, people who sail abroad or engage in other kinds of business do not want what they are doing at the time; who would want to run the risk of sailing and the troubles of business? What they want, I imagine, is the object of their voyage, to make a fortune; it is wealth that they sail abroad for. d
POLUS: Certainly.
SOCRATES: And isn't this true in every case? When someone performs an act as a means to an end, he wants not his act, but the object of his act.
POLUS: Yes. e
SOCRATES: Now, is there anything which is not either good or bad or intermediate and neither good nor bad?
POLUS: There can be nothing else, Socrates.
SOCRATES: Would you call wisdom and health and riches and the like good, and their opposites bad?
POLUS: I would.
SOCRATES: And would you place in the intermediate class such things as the following, which partake sometimes of the nature of good, sometimes of bad, and sometimes of neither;

468 I mean, for example, sitting and walking and running and sailing, or, to take things of a different type, wood and stone and the like? Are these what you mean when you say that some things are neither good nor bad?

POLUS: Precisely.

SOCRATES: Now, do men perform these neutral acts as a means to the good, or vice versa?

POLUS: The former, of course.

b SOCRATES: Then when we walk we walk as a means to the good, because we think it is the better course; and when we stand still, on the other hand, we stand still from the same motive as a means to the good. Do you agree?

POLUS: Yes.

SOCRATES: And when we kill or banish or confiscate, if we ever do so, we act from a belief that it is better for us to do so than not?

POLUS: Certainly.

SOCRATES: Then people do all these things as a means to the good?

POLUS: Yes.

SOCRATES: We agreed, didn't we, that we do not want acts that are means, but the ends to which they are means?

c POLUS: Of course.

SOCRATES: So we do not want to slaughter or cause banishment or confiscate property simply for its own sake; we want them if they bring advantage, but not if they are harmful. As you say yourself, we want what is good, we do not want what is intermediate, still less what is bad. Am I right, Polus, or not? Why don't you answer?

POLUS: You are right.

d SOCRATES: Then, if we agree on this, when a tyrant or an orator kills or banishes or confiscates property because he believes it to be better for him, and it turns out to be worse, we must allow that he does what seems fitting for him, mustn't we?

POLUS: Yes.

SOCRATES: But does he do what he *wants*, if what he does turns out to be bad? Why don't you answer?

POLUS: I agree that he doesn't do what he wants.

SOCRATES: How can one say then that such a man has great power in his city, when by your own admission great power is a great good for its possessor? e

POLUS: One can't.

SOCRATES: So it appears that I was right when I said that a man might do what seems fitting to him in a city without either having great power or doing what he really wants.

One might argue that Polus agrees too readily with Socrates' separation of means and ends in this section; the distinction does not have to be so clear cut, since what I want might be either a means or an end, depending on how I choose to describe it. For example, if I choose painful dental treatment as a cure for toothache, I might say that I do want the means, or even if, strictly speaking I don't, I have chosen these *means, rather than any other, to the desired end, i.e. relief from pain. The separation of means and ends might also seem artificial in another sense, for example, if I walk rather than drive to work, I am choosing a means to a desired end, namely getting to work; but in this example, the so-called means may also be part of the end – the enjoyment of walking (rather than driving). On the significance of how an act or experience is described, i.e. as a means or an end, see Irwin 1979, p. 145; Vlastos 1991, pp. 150 ff., Beversluis 2000, pp. 325 ff.*

B[3] 468e6–471d2

Socrates and Polus speak briefly at cross-purposes (468e6–469b7) until Socrates reveals the belief which underlies his side of the exchange, the explanation of which becomes the subject of the rest of the dialogue with Polus: 'it is better to suffer than to do wrong' (469b8 ff.). In saying it is 'better' to suffer, Socrates means better for (i.e. more to the advantage of) the victim than the doer. So the wrongdoer is more miserable (less well-off) than the victim. This belief would have seemed more outrageously paradoxical to Plato's contemporaries than to a post-Christian world; in another dialogue, Meno, *Plato puts into the mouth of Meno the conventional Greek view: 'the excellence of a man . . . is to do good to his friends, bad to his enemies and to take care to come to no harm himself' (*Meno *71e). To suffer injury without being able or willing to defend oneself was a sign of weakness; the power to avenge oneself on enemies was to be respected. In response to Socrates, Polus invokes what he considers a decisive refutation by citing an extreme example of the* adikos eudaimon, *the 'happy wrongdoer'.* Eudaimon *has a more objective connotation than the English translation 'happy' implies; it means, rather, 'fortunate' or 'prosperous', literally = 'having a good destiny (*daimon*)', as in the famous Greek proverb 'Count no man happy until he is dead'. The problem of the evil person who seemed to prosper was one which fascinated and preoccupied Greek moralists; some popular solutions included the belief that retribution would finally catch up with evil-doers during their lifetime, or after death, or even be passed on to future generations. Socrates' solution, that the wrongdoer is himself not really* eudaimon *at all, is argued in the rest of the dialogue with Polus (see especially B[6] below and also in the myth of the afterlife at the end of the whole dialogue, C[12]).*

POLUS: To listen to you, Socrates, one might think that you wouldn't be glad to have the opportunity of doing what you think fitting in the city rather than not, and that you don't feel envy when you see a man who can kill or rob or imprison anyone he thinks fit.

SOCRATES: Justly or unjustly, do you mean?

469 POLUS: It makes no difference; he's enviable in either case, isn't he?

SOCRATES: Take care what you are saying, Polus!

POLUS: Why?

SOCRATES: Because you shouldn't speak like this of people who are unenviable or miserable; they are rather to be pitied.

POLUS: Do you really believe that about the people I am speaking of?

SOCRATES: Of course.

POLUS: You think that someone who decides to kill, and kills rightly, is miserable and pitiable?

SOCRATES: No, but I don't call him enviable.

POLUS: A moment ago, you called him miserable, didn't you?

SOCRATES: I meant the person who kills wrongfully, my friend. b Him I call pitiable as well as miserable. But I don't envy the individual who kills with right on his side.

POLUS: Doubtless a man who is put to death wrongfully is pitiable and miserable!

SOCRATES: Less so than the man who kills him, Polus, or the man who is put to death because he deserves it.

POLUS: How so, Socrates?

SOCRATES: Because the greatest of all misfortunes is to do wrong.

POLUS: That is the greatest? Surely it is worse to suffer wrong?

SOCRATES: Certainly not.

POLUS: Do you mean to say that you would rather suffer wrong than do wrong?

SOCRATES: I would rather avoid both; but if I had to choose c one or the other I would rather suffer wrong than do wrong.

POLUS: Then you wouldn't choose to be a tyrant?

SOCRATES: I certainly wouldn't if your notion of a tyrant is the same as mine.

POLUS: I mean by a tyrant, I repeat, a man who can do whatever he decides in the state, killing and banishing and having his own way in everything.

SOCRATES: My good friend, hear what I have to say and then raise objections. Suppose I were to meet you in a crowded d market-place with a dagger under my arm, and say, 'Polus, I've just acquired a simply wonderful instrument of tyranny. Such is my power in this city that if I decide that any of the people you see around you should die on the spot, die they shall; or if I decide that any of them ought to have their head broken or clothes torn, it's as good as done.' If on top of that, to convince you, I were to display my dagger, you would e probably reply: 'At that rate, Socrates, anybody can exercise great power; houses can be burnt down on a whim, and the dockyards and triremes of the Athenian navy and all the merchant ships in public and private ownership.' So it appears that doing what one decides is not the same as having great power, is it?

POLUS: Not in this case, certainly.

470 SOCRATES: Can you tell me what the flaw is in this kind of power?

POLUS: Yes.

SOCRATES: What is it then?

POLUS: It is that a man who behaves like this is bound to be punished.

SOCRATES: And being punished is an evil?

POLUS: Of course.

SOCRATES: Then, my good friend, you come back again to the conclusion that if doing what one decides on means acting beneficially, then it is a good thing and this, I think, is to have great power; otherwise it is a bad and feeble thing. Let's look b at the matter in this light. We agreed, didn't we, that with regard to the actions we mentioned just now, killing and banishing and robbing, it is sometimes better to do them and sometimes not?

POLUS: Certainly.

SOCRATES: Then here, it seems, we have one point on which we are agreed?

POLUS: Yes.

SOCRATES: Can you tell when it is better to do these things? How do you draw the line?

POLUS: No, you answer that yourself, Socrates.

c SOCRATES: Then I'll tell you, Polus, if it is pleasanter to hear it from me. I should say that when these actions are right it is better, and when they are wrong, the reverse.

POLUS: You're a hard man to get the better of, Socrates, but couldn't even a child prove that you are mistaken here?

SOCRATES: Then I shall be very grateful to the child, and equally so to you, if you will show me my mistake and cure me of my silliness. Don't be backward in doing a kindness to a friend. Prove me wrong.

POLUS: I can do that, Socrates, without resorting to ancient history. The events of only the other day are enough to refute you and to show that many wrongdoers are happy. d

SOCRATES: What events do you mean?

POLUS: Well, look at that fellow Archelaus the son of Perdiccas ruling in Macedonia.[44]

SOCRATES: I've heard of him anyhow, even if I can't look at him.

POLUS: Do you think that he is happy or miserable?

SOCRATES: I don't know, Polus; I've never met the man.

POLUS: Do you mean that you can't tell at once even from this distance, without meeting him, that he is happy? e

SOCRATES: By Zeus, indeed I can't.

POLUS: Then no doubt you'll say even of the Great King[45] that you don't know whether he is happy, Socrates.

SOCRATES: It will be no more than the truth; I don't know what degree of education and righteousness he has attained.

POLUS: What? Does happiness depend entirely on that?

SOCRATES: Yes, Polus, in my opinion it does; I maintain that a man and a woman are happy if they are honourable and good,[46] but miserable if they are vicious and wicked.

POLUS: Then by your account, this Archelaus is miserable. 471

SOCRATES: If he is a wrongdoer, my friend, certainly.

POLUS: Of course he's a wrongdoer. He had no claim to the throne he now possesses, for his mother was a slave of Alcetas the brother of Perdiccas, and by rights he too was Alcetas' slave; if he had chosen to follow the path of virtue he would be Alcetas' slave still and, according to you, happy. But as things are he is amazingly miserable, because he has committed enormous crimes. First of all, he sent for this same Alcetas, who was his uncle as well as his master, on the pretence that he would surrender to him the throne of which Perdiccas had deprived him. When he had entertained him and made him drunk, together with his son Alexander, who was his cousin and almost the same age as himself, he flung them both into a cart and took them out by night and murdered them, so that neither of them were ever heard of again. So far was he from repenting of these crimes and realizing that he had become utterly miserable that shortly afterwards b c he refused another chance to make himself happy. He had a brother, Perdiccas' legitimate son, a child about seven years old, whom duty required that he should bring up and place on the throne. Instead he threw him into a well and drowned him, and told his mother Cleopatra that the child had fallen into the well and been killed while he was running after a goose. So now, as the greatest criminal in the country, far from being the happiest Macedonian alive, he is the most miserable, and no doubt there are a number of Athenians, d beginning with you, who would prefer to be any Macedonian, however obscure, rather than Archelaus.[47]

B[4] 471d3–472d1

Another short interlude in the discussion (see A[5] above) which consists of a reflection by Socrates on its conduct, as opposed to its content. What constitutes proof that one's assertions are true? Polus relies on oratory (as in his previous speech, 471a4 ff.) and the support of numbers, whereas Socrates only acknowledges the validity of argument, against which weight and eminence of supporters are irrelevant. In the elaborate calling of hypothetical 'witnesses' for Polus (471e2 ff.), Socrates lays particular emphasis on his own social and intellectual isolation in Athens.

On the distinction between validity and truth, see the Introduction, 'Structure and argument'.

SOCRATES: I said at the beginning of our conversation, Polus, that while I thought you admirably well trained in oratory you seemed to me to have neglected the art of reasoning. Is this really the argument by which a child could prove and by which in your opinion *you* have now proved that I was wrong when I said that a bad man is not happy? How can this be, my good fellow, seeing that I don't admit the force of anything that you have said?

e POLUS: Won't admit it, you mean; you really believe I am right.

SOCRATES: The fact is, my dear friend, that you are trying to prove me wrong by the use of oratory, like people in the law courts. They think there that they have got the better of the other party whenever they can produce many respectable witnesses to what they say, while their opponent can produce only one or none at all. But this kind of proof is useless in establishing the truth, for it can easily happen that a man is 472 overborne by the false evidence of many apparently respectable persons. And now, in your present case, practically the whole population of Athens, Athenians and foreigners alike, will agree with you that I am not speaking the truth, if you like to call them as witnesses; you can, if you wish, get the support of Nicias the son of Niceratus and his brothers, who have a row of tripods standing to their credit in the precinct of Dionysus;[48] you can get Aristocrates[49] the son of Scellius, b who dedicated that splendid offering in the sanctuary of Pythian Apollo, you can get the whole family of Pericles[50] or any other Athenian family that you care to choose. But I, though I am but a single individual, do not agree with you, for you produce no compelling reason why I should; instead you call numerous false witnesses against me in your attempt to evict me from my lawful property, the truth.[51] I believe that nothing worth speaking of will have been accomplished in our discussion unless I can obtain your agreement, and yours alone, as a witness to the truth of what I say; and the same c holds good for you, in my opinion; unless you can get just me, me only, on your side you can disregard what the rest of the world may say.

There are then these two sorts of proof, the kind on which you and many other people rely and the kind which I on my side think reliable. Let us compare them and see how they differ, for the subject of our argument, so far from being trivial, is perhaps that on which knowledge is finest and ignorance most shameful; it is, in brief, knowledge or ignorance of who is happy and who is not.

B[5] 472d1–476a2

Socrates asserts another paradox, closely based on the first (see B[3] above) – that (if it is worse to do than to suffer wrong) the wrongdoer will be more miserable (opposite of eudaimon*) if he does not suffer punishment, a proposition which Polus dismisses as self-evidently 'absurd' (*atopon *473a1), and once again gives extreme examples of what he considers the absurdity of Socrates' assertion (473b12 ff.). Socrates then embarks on the proof of his contention that it is worse to do than to suffer wrong. He secures from Polus a key admission: that although doing wrong is 'better' than suffering wrong, it is nevertheless 'more shameful' (474c8). Socrates then takes advantage of the wide range of meaning attached to 'shameful' (*aischron*) and its opposite 'fine' (*kalon*) to make a polar distinction based on a number of examples taken from objects of the senses and from laws and behaviour: what is fine must be* either *useful or pleasant; what is shameful must be* either *harmful* or *painful. So what is 'more shameful' (i.e. more* aischron*) must be either more painful or more harmful; it is self-evidently not more painful, so it must be the other alternative, i.e. more harmful. So, since Polus has admitted that doing wrong is more shameful than suffering wrong, doing wrong must actually be more harmful (i.e. worse). If, conversely, it is 'finer' (i.e. more* kalon*) to suffer wrong, it must be the opposite of 'more shameful', i.e. either more useful or more pleasant; it is self-evidently not more pleasant to suffer wrong, so it follows that it must be more useful (i.e. better). Polus is refuted.*

d SOCRATES: First of all, to take the point which is at issue at the moment, you believe that it is possible for a man to be happy who is wicked and is a wrongdoer, since you believe Archelaus to be wicked but happy. Am I right in taking that to be your position?

POLUS: Absolutely right.

SOCRATES: And I say that it is impossible. Our disagreement turns on this single point. Good. Now what I want to know is this: will a man who does wrong be happy if he is brought to justice and punished?

POLUS: On the contrary, he will then be most miserable.

SOCRATES: But, by your account, if the wrongdoer isn't brought to justice he will be happy? e

POLUS: Yes.

SOCRATES: On the other hand, Polus, my opinion is that the wrongdoer, the criminal, is miserable in any case, but more miserable if he does not pay the penalty and suffer punishment for his crimes, and less miserable if he does pay the penalty and suffer punishment at the hands of gods and men.

POLUS: What an absurd proposition to maintain, Socrates. 473

SOCRATES: I will try nevertheless to make you also concur in this view, my friend, for I have a high regard for you. At the moment the point on which we differ is this – see if you agree. I said earlier, didn't I, that doing wrong is worse than suffering wrong?[52]

POLUS: You did.

SOCRATES: And you said that suffering wrong is worse.

POLUS: Yes.

SOCRATES: And I said that wrongdoers are miserable, and you denied it.

POLUS: Yes, by Zeus!

SOCRATES: That is your opinion, Polus. b

POLUS: And a true opinion too.

SOCRATES: Maybe. You said also that wrongdoers are happy if they escape punishment.

POLUS: Of course.

SOCRATES: But I said that they are the most miserable of men, and that those who are punished are less so. Would you care to refute this proposition?

POLUS: That is an even harder task than you set me before, Socrates.

SOCRATES: Not hard, Polus, but impossible; truth can never be refuted.

POLUS: What do you mean? If a person is arrested for the crime c of plotting a tyranny and racked and castrated and blinded with hot irons, and finally, after suffering many other varieties of terrible torture and seeing his wife and children suffer the same, is crucified or burnt at the stake, will this person be happier than if he gets off, establishes himself as tyrant and spends the rest of his life in power in the city doing whatever d he wants, envied and called happy by citizens and foreigners alike? Is this what you maintain that it is impossible to prove untrue?

SOCRATES: You're trying to frighten me with bogeys,[53] my good Polus. You're no more proving me wrong than you were just now, when you appealed to witnesses. Just remind me of a small point: did you say 'arrested for the crime of plotting a tyranny'?

POLUS: Yes.

SOCRATES: Well, neither the man who establishes a tyranny wrongfully nor the man who is punished for attempting to do so can ever be described as the happier; you can't compare e the happiness of two people who are both miserable. But the man who gets away with it and becomes a tyrant is the more miserable. What's this, Polus? Laughing? Is this a new type of proof, laughing at what your opponent says instead of giving reasons?

POLUS: Do you suppose that reasons are needed, Socrates, when you say things that no one else in the world would say? Ask any of our friends here.

SOCRATES: I'm no politician, my dear Polus. Only last year 474 when I was chosen by lot to be a member of the Council and my tribe was presiding, I had to put a question to the vote, and provoked laughter by my ignorance of the correct procedure.[54] Don't ask me to repeat that experience now by taking the votes of the present company, but, if you have no better proof to advance, do as I suggested just now and put yourself in my hands as I put myself in yours; have a taste of the sort of proof that I believe in.

My method is to call in support of my statements the evidence of a single witness, the man I am arguing with, and to take his vote alone; the rest of the world are nothing to me; I am not talking to them. See now if you are prepared to b submit yourself in your turn to examination by answering my questions. I maintain that you and the world in general, as well as I, consider doing wrong worse than suffering wrong, and not being punished worse than being punished.

POLUS: And I say that neither I nor anyone else believes such a thing. Would *you* rather suffer wrong than do wrong?

SOCRATES: Yes, and so would you and so would everybody.

POLUS: On the contrary, neither you nor I nor anybody would make that choice.

SOCRATES: Well, will you answer my questions? c

POLUS: Certainly, I am eager to know what on earth you will say.

SOCRATES: If you want to know, answer as if we were beginning again at the beginning. Which do you think is worse, Polus, doing wrong or suffering wrong?

POLUS: I think suffering wrong.

SOCRATES: And which do you think the more shameful thing, doing wrong or suffering wrong? Answer.

POLUS: Doing wrong.

SOCRATES: If it is more shameful, isn't it also worse?

POLUS: Not at all.

SOCRATES: I see. Then you don't consider good identical with fine, or bad with shameful? d

POLUS: No, I don't.

SOCRATES: What about this, then? Have you no standard to which you refer when you apply the word fine to any fine thing, whether it is a body or a colour or a shape or a voice or a mode of behaviour? Take physical beauty first. When you call a body fine are you not referring either to its usefulness for some particular purpose or to some feeling of pleasure which makes glad the eyes of its beholders? Is there any reason other than these for calling a body fine?

POLUS: No. e

SOCRATES: And similarly with the other things, shapes and colours. You call them fine, don't you, because they are either pleasant or useful or both?

POLUS: Yes.

SOCRATES: And is the same true of voices and musical sounds in general?

POLUS: Yes.

SOCRATES: Now, with regard to laws and modes of behaviour; their fineness also presumably depends on their being either useful or pleasant or both.

POLUS: I agree.

475 SOCRATES: And shall we say the same about the fineness of various branches of knowledge?

POLUS: Certainly; your use of pleasure and good[55] as criteria of fineness is now excellent, Socrates.

SOCRATES: Then we must define what is shameful by the opposites of these, that is to say by pain and evil.

POLUS: Unquestionably.

SOCRATES: So whenever we call one of two fine things the finer, we mean that it surpasses the other either in one or both of these qualities; it is either more pleasant or more useful or both.

POLUS: Certainly.

SOCRATES: And whenever one of two shameful things is the more shameful, it must be because it is either more painful or b more evil or both. Do you agree?

POLUS: Yes.

SOCRATES: Now then: what did we say a moment ago about doing and suffering wrong? You said, I think, that suffering wrong was the greater evil, but doing wrong more shameful.

POLUS: I did.

SOCRATES: Then if doing wrong is more shameful than suffering wrong, its greater shamefulness must inevitably consist in its being either more painful or more evil or both? Isn't that inevitable?

POLUS: Certainly.

c SOCRATES: First, then, let us consider whether doing wrong exceeds suffering wrong in pain. Do those who do wrong feel more pain than those who suffer wrong?

POLUS: Most certainly not.

SOCRATES: Then doing wrong does not exceed in pain?

POLUS: No.

SOCRATES: And if it is not more painful, it cannot exceed in both.

POLUS: Of course not.

SOCRATES: Then only the third possibility is left.

POLUS: Yes.

SOCRATES: That is, that it is more evil.

POLUS: So it seems.

SOCRATES: Then since it involves greater evil, doing wrong will be worse than suffering wrong.

POLUS: Obviously.

SOCRATES: Didn't you and I agree before with the opinion of most people that doing wrong is a more shameful thing than suffering wrong? d

POLUS: Yes.

SOCRATES: And now it turns out to be a greater evil as well.

POLUS: Apparently.

SOCRATES: Would you then prefer a greater degree of evil and shamefulness to a lesser? Don't be afraid to answer, Polus; it won't hurt you. Be a man and submit to the argument as you would to a doctor, and answer 'yes' or 'no' to my question. e

POLUS: My answer is 'no' then, Socrates.

SOCRATES: Would anybody prefer it?

POLUS: I don't think so, according to this argument anyway.

SOCRATES: I was right then when I said that neither you nor I nor anyone would prefer doing wrong to suffering wrong, since the former turns out to be the greater evil.

POLUS: So it appears.

SOCRATES: You see then, Polus, that when our two methods of proving our points are compared, they bear no resemblance to each other. Whereas you have everybody in agreement with you except me, I am content if I can get just your agreement and testimony; if I can get your one vote I care nothing for those of the rest of the world. 476

Socrates owes his initial success with this rather contrived symmetrical argument to:

1. Polus' fatal admission at 474c8 that doing wrong is 'more shameful' than suffering wrong; why does Polus, having steadfastly denied that doing wrong is worse, a greater evil, than suffering wrong, concede this crucial point? The answer, as

Callicles later realizes (see C[1] below), is that while Polus, like most Athenians, may believe that doing wrong is more profitable to the doer (i.e. 'better'), Socrates' introduction of the idea of 'shameful', which includes notions of honour and dishonour, forces the conventional Polus to consider 'doing wrong' from another angle – the status of the wrongdoer in the eyes of the community. It might secretly approve of such a person, but, in public, notions of honour and dishonour tended to prevail. Socrates takes advantage of this ambivalent attitude.

2. Socrates' subsequent polar definitions of 'fine' and 'shameful'; these also draw on conventional meanings of these words: kalon *has a close association with the pleasure of experiencing sight, sound etc., as well as with what is* ophelimon *('useful'), which makes plausible the move to define its polar opposite (*aischron*) in terms of the opposite qualities (pain and harm). However, a third possibility is a definition of* kalon *in a moral sense, as 'good', 'noble' or 'honourable', an equally acceptable definition in ordinary discourse. Polus does not stop to consider whether the definitions of* kalon/aischron *'pushed on' him by Socrates really exhaust the possibilities.*

A more philosophically acute Polus might also have fought back at 474e ff. by asking: for whom is doing/suffering wrong more painful/pleasant or fine/useful? For those concerned – the community – or for the immediate subject? If the community, Socrates' argument would fail, since one side of the polar definition cannot be so easily eliminated: doing wrong might well be more painful for those other than the doer, for example the community, who witness it. But Polus doesn't ask for clarification and so Socrates gets a free run with this argument.

It is worth noting that it is at the start of this passage of argument, which is crucial for Polus' whole case, that he turns (rather suddenly for dramatic verisimilitude?) from a contentious and derisive opponent into a submissive 'yes-man'.

The argument in this section has attracted much attention from commentators, and the question whether Polus is really refuted by Socrates has been disputed. See e.g. Vlastos 1967; Kahn 1983, pp. 86–92; Santas 1979, pp. 236 ff.; Beversluis 2000, p. 328.

B[6] 476a2–481b5

Socrates now returns to the first paradox which he left unresolved at the beginning of B[5]: that it is a greater evil to escape punishment for wrongdoing than to be punished for it. He establishes (476b3 ff.) that an object of action suffers in the same way as the agent acts: for example, if something is done violently the object of the action suffers violently; so, if someone punishes, and they punish justly, then the person punished is punished justly. What is just is fine; so the person punished has a fine thing done to him. What is fine is good, i.e. either pleasant (which, on the argument of B[5] above, can in this case be eliminated) or useful. Good is useful and beneficial, so the punished man receives a benefit. This sequence depends largely on positions established previously (in B[5] above) and relies again on the ambiguity of the reference to value-terms. The slide, from saying that X does something good to Y to saying that what is done to Y is good for him, *goes undetected by Polus.*

However Socrates then, with apparent casualness, introduces a new element into the argument – the soul (477a7). Earlier (B[1] above) Socrates had without question divided arts into those concerning the body and those concerning the soul (on the soul in Plato and Greek thought generally, see the Introduction, 'The issues of the dialogue'). Here Socrates relies on two further unquestioned assumptions: 1. that there is a close analogy between the behaviour of the soul and the body, e.g. just as medicine cures diseases of the body, so just punishment cures badness in the soul; 2. that what happens to the soul (good or evil) is more important than what happens to the body; wickedness (which pertains to the soul) is more shameful (i.e. worse) than poverty or disease (which pertain to the body).

Socrates then re-runs the argument of B[5] for the third time (477c6 ff.) to demonstrate that badness of soul is the 'greatest evil that exists' (477e5–6). Then, by analogy, just as the art of medicine cures the physically sick, so justice cures someone with badness of soul. And just as being cured of a physical disease is better for the sick individual than being allowed to suffer untreated, so, by analogy, being punished for wickedness is better for the individual than going unpunished – indeed, since what happens to the soul is more important than what happens to the body, going unpunished for wrongdoing is the worst of all possible evils to befall anyone. So the apparently adikos eudaimon *('prosperous wrongdoer'), like the tyrant Archelaus (see B[3] above), by escaping unpunished is actually in the worst possible state ('miserable above all other men' 479e3–4). Socrates concludes by suggesting therefore that it is not only self-evidently in the interest of a wrongdoer to submit himself to punishment (just as a sick man goes to the doctor), but that we have an opportunity to do our enemies the worst of all injuries by ensuring that they escape punishment! This final suggestion, which follows logically from the previous argument, but which is clearly a piece of 'comic fantasy' (Dodds 1959, p. 259), leads to the incredulous intervention of Callicles, which marks the start of the long third and final section of the dialogue.*

SOCRATES: So much then for that; now let us consider the second point on which we were at issue, whether being punished for one's wrongdoing is the greatest of evils, as you thought, or whether not being punished is a greater evil, which was my opinion. Let's look at it like this. Would you say that paying the penalty for wrongdoing is the same thing as being justly punished?

POLUS: Yes.

b SOCRATES: So can you maintain that what is just[56] is not always fine in so far as it is just? Think well before you answer.

POLUS: I think it is, Socrates.

SOCRATES: Next take this question. If someone does something, must there be something which is the object of the action?

POLUS: I think so.

SOCRATES: Does what the object has done to it correspond in nature and quality to the act of the agent? For example, if someone strikes, something must be struck, mustn't it?

POLUS: Inevitably.

SOCRATES: And if the agent strikes violently or quickly the object must be struck in the same way?

POLUS: Yes. c

SOCRATES: The effect on the object of the stroke is qualified in the same way as the act of the striker?

POLUS: Of course.

SOCRATES: Again, if someone causes burning, must there be something being burnt?

POLUS: Naturally.

SOCRATES: And if the burning is violent or painful, what is burnt must be burnt in the corresponding way?

POLUS: Certainly.

SOCRATES: And does the same hold good if a cut is made? Something is cut?

POLUS: Yes.

SOCRATES: And if the cut is big or deep or painful, the object which is cut receives a cut corresponding in kind to what the d agent inflicts?

POLUS: It seems so.

SOCRATES: To sum up, do you agree with what I said a moment ago, that what the object has done to it is qualified in the same way as what the agent does?[57]

POLUS: I agree.

SOCRATES: Then, if that is granted, is being punished active or passive?

POLUS: Passive, Socrates, of course.

SOCRATES: Then there must be a corresponding agent?

POLUS: Obviously; the man who inflicts the punishment.

SOCRATES: Does a man who punishes rightly punish justly? e

POLUS: Yes.

SOCRATES: And is his action just or unjust?

POLUS: Just.

SOCRATES: Then the man who is punished, paying the penalty, suffers justly?

POLUS: It seems so.

SOCRATES: And we have agreed that what is just is fine?

POLUS: Certainly.

SOCRATES: Then the man who punishes does a fine thing, and the man who is punished has a fine thing done to him.[58]

POLUS: Yes.

477 SOCRATES: And if fine, good, since it must be either pleasant or useful.

POLUS: Inevitably.

SOCRATES: Then the treatment received by the man who is punished is good?

POLUS: Apparently.

SOCRATES: Then it must be useful, a benefit, to him?

POLUS: Yes.

SOCRATES: And is the benefit what I take it to be, that if he is justly punished his soul is improved?

POLUS: Probably.

SOCRATES: Then the man who is punished is freed from evil in the soul?

POLUS: Yes.

SOCRATES: In that case, is he not freed from the greatest of all b evils? Look at it this way: where a man's material fortune is concerned, can you name any evil except poverty?

POLUS: No.

SOCRATES: And what of his physical constitution? Wouldn't you say that evil here means weakness and disease and deformity and the like?

POLUS: Yes.

SOCRATES: Now, do you recognize the existence of such a thing as an evil state of the soul?

POLUS: Of course.

SOCRATES: Do you mean by this wickedness and ignorance and cowardice and so on?

POLUS: Certainly.

c SOCRATES: Then in these three things, possessions, body and soul, you recognize three corresponding bad states, poverty, disease and wickedness?

POLUS: Yes.

SOCRATES: Now, which of these three bad states is the most shameful? Is it not wrongdoing and badness of soul in general?

POLUS: Certainly.

SOCRATES: And if it is the most shameful, is it not the worst?

POLUS: What do you mean, Socrates?

SOCRATES: Simply this. We agreed before that in any comparison of shamefulness the first place must be assigned to what produces either the greatest pain or the greatest harm or both.

POLUS: Agreed.

SOCRATES: And we have now agreed on the supreme shamefulness of wrongdoing and all badness of soul?

POLUS: Yes, it has been agreed. d

SOCRATES: Then its supreme shamefulness must be due to its being either surpassingly painful or surpassingly harmful, or both?

POLUS: It must.

SOCRATES: Now, are wickedness and excess and cowardice and ignorance more painful than poverty and sickness?

POLUS: Nothing in our discussion leads me to think so, Socrates.

SOCRATES: Then since by your own admission badness of soul is not supremely painful, it must owe its superiority in shamefulness over other kinds of badness to the fact that it produces an amazing degree of harm and evil. e

POLUS: It would seem so.

SOCRATES: I suppose that what produces the greatest harm must be the greatest evil in the world?

POLUS: Yes.

SOCRATES: Then wrongdoing and excess and other kinds of wickedness of soul are the greatest evil that exists?

POLUS: Apparently.

SOCRATES: Now, what is the art which relieves a man from poverty? Isn't it the art of making money?

POLUS: Yes.

SOCRATES: And what cures disease? Isn't it the art of medicine?

POLUS: Of course.

SOCRATES: Then what is the art which cures wickedness and wrongdoing? If you are at a loss for an answer when it is put like that, look at it in this way. Where do we take sufferers from physical ailments? 478

POLUS: To the doctor, Socrates.

SOCRATES: And those who are wicked and licentious?

POLUS: To the judges, do you mean?

SOCRATES: To be punished?

POLUS: Yes.

SOCRATES: Do not those who punish rightly employ some kind of justice in doing so?

POLUS: Obviously.

SOCRATES: Then money-making cures poverty, medicine b disease, and justice excess and wrongdoing.

POLUS: So it seems.

SOCRATES: Now, which of these is the finest?

POLUS: Which of what?

SOCRATES: Money-making, medicine and justice.

POLUS: Justice, Socrates, by a long way.

SOCRATES: If it is the finest, must it not produce either the greatest pleasure or the greatest benefit or both?

POLUS: Yes.

SOCRATES: Is medical treatment pleasant? Do people like being in the hands of doctors?

POLUS: Not in my opinion.

SOCRATES: But it is beneficial, isn't it?

POLUS: Yes.

c SOCRATES: It relieves a person from a great evil so that it is worthwhile undergoing the pain to regain one's health.

POLUS: Of course.

SOCRATES: Physically speaking, which is the happier condition, to be cured by a doctor or never to be ill at all?

POLUS: Obviously, never to be ill at all.

SOCRATES: Then happiness, it seems, consists not so much in being relieved of evil as in never acquiring it in the first place.

POLUS: Yes.

d SOCRATES: Well, how about this? If two people have a disease, whether in body or soul, which is the more miserable: the one who undergoes treatment and is cured of his evil, or the one who has no treatment and continues to suffer?

POLUS: I suppose the person who has no treatment.

SOCRATES: Didn't we agree that to be punished is to be cured of the worst of all evils, wickedness?

POLUS: Yes.

SOCRATES: Because justice presumably teaches people self-control, makes them better and is the cure for wickedness.

POLUS: Yes.

SOCRATES: Then the happiest is the person who has no badness in his soul, since this has been shown to be the worst of all bad things.

POLUS: Clearly. e

SOCRATES: And the next happiest, I suppose, is the person who is cured.

POLUS: Apparently.

SOCRATES: That is to say, the one who undergoes reproof and chastisement and is punished for his faults.

POLUS: Yes.

SOCRATES: And the worst is the life of the person who continues in wrongdoing and is not cured.

POLUS: It appears so.

SOCRATES: But isn't he precisely the one who commits the greatest crimes and indulges in the greatest wrongdoing and yet manages never to suffer reproof and punishment and retribution; the man in fact who behaves just as you say Archelaus has behaved and all the other tyrants and orators 479 and potentates?

POLUS: So it seems.

SOCRATES: Their achievements, it would appear, my good friend, are comparable to those of someone suffering from the most serious illnesses, who manages to avoid giving any account of his physical defects to the doctors and undergoing treatment, because, like a child, he is afraid of the pain involved in cautery and surgery. Don't you agree? b

POLUS: Yes.

SOCRATES: Because he is presumably ignorant of the nature of health and physical well-being. And the agreement which we have now reached, Polus, points to the conclusion that those who flee from justice are in a similar condition; they see the pain which punishment involves but are blind to its benefits and do not realize that to live with an unhealthy body is a far less miserable fate than the companionship of an unhealthy c soul, one that is rotten, wicked and impure. So they strain every nerve to escape punishment and to avoid being cured of the worst of all evils; for this purpose they procure wealth and friends and make themselves as persuasive speakers as they can. But if we are right in what we have agreed, Polus, do you see what conclusions follow from the argument? Or would you prefer that we just sum them up?

POLUS: If you think so.

SOCRATES: First, it emerges that wickedness and wrongdoing are the greatest evil. Do you agree?

d POLUS: It seems so, at any rate.

SOCRATES: Next, has it not been demonstrated that being punished is a way of deliverance from this evil?

POLUS: It looks like it.

SOCRATES: And that not being punished renders the evil permanent?

POLUS: Yes.

SOCRATES: Then acting wrongly stands only second in the list of evil things. The first and greatest of all is not to be punished for one's wrongdoing.

POLUS: Apparently so.

SOCRATES: And wasn't this exactly the point at issue between us, my friend? You thought Archelaus happy for committing

e the greatest crimes with impunity, and I was of the contrary opinion and maintained that Archelaus or anyone else who escapes punishment for his wrongdoing must be miserable above all other men, and that as a general rule the man who does wrong is more miserable than the man who is wronged, and the man who escapes punishment more miserable than the man who receives it. Wasn't that what I said?

POLUS: Yes.

SOCRATES: And hasn't it been demonstrated that what was said was true?

POLUS: So it appears.

SOCRATES: Well then, Polus, if this is indeed true, where is the

480 great use of oratory? Doesn't it follow from our agreements now that a man's duty is to keep himself from doing wrong, because he will otherwise bring plenty of evil upon himself?

POLUS: Certainly.

SOCRATES: And if he or anyone he cares for does wrong, he ought of his own accord to go where he will most quickly be punished, to the judge, that is, as he would to a doctor, eager to prevent the disease of wrongdoing from becoming chronic and causing his soul to fester till it is incurable. What else can b we say, Polus, if our previous conclusions hold good? Doesn't it inevitably follow that nothing else will be consistent with them?

POLUS: Yes indeed, for what else can we say, Socrates?

SOCRATES: Then we shall have no use for oratory, Polus, as a means of defence either for our own wrongdoing or for those of our parents or friends or children or country. It may however be of service if one adopts the contrary view and holds it to be a man's duty to denounce himself in the first c place and next any of his family or friends who may at any time do wrong, bringing the crime out of concealment into the light of day in order that the wrongdoer may be punished and regain his health. Such a man must force himself and others not to play the coward, but to submit to the law with closed eyes like a man, as one would to surgery or cautery, ignoring the pain for the sake of the good and fine result which it will bring. Whatever the punishment that the crime deserves he must offer himself to it cheerfully, if flogging to be flogged, if imprisonment to go to prison, if a fine to pay d up, if exile then to depart, if death then to die. He must be the first to accuse himself and members of his family, and the use that he will make of oratory will be to ensure that by having their misdeeds brought to light, wrongdoers are delivered from the supreme evil of wrongdoing. Are we to agree with that line of conduct, Polus, or not?

POLUS: It sounds absurd to me, Socrates, but I suppose that it e is consistent with our previous discussion.

SOCRATES: Then must we not either upset the conclusions we have already reached or accept that they necessarily follow?

POLUS: Yes, that is so.

SOCRATES: Then again, take the converse situation. Suppose that it is ever right for us to inflict injury on an enemy or on anyone else, provided of course that we run no risk of being injured ourselves by the enemy – that is a point one must be on one's guard against. On that hypothesis, if the enemy injures a third party, one must clearly make every effort, both 481 in speech and action, to prevent his being brought to book and coming before the judge at all; if that is impossible one must contrive that the enemy gets off unpunished. If he has stolen a lot of money, he must not pay it back, but keep it and spend it on himself and his family without regard to god or man; if he has committed crimes for which the penalty is death, he must not be executed. The most desirable thing would be that he should never die, but live for ever in an immortality of crime; the next best that he should live as long b as possible in that condition. To ensure that result, Polus, I allow that oratory might be of service, since it seems to me unlikely to be of much use to a man who is not going to do wrong. That is, supposing that it has any use at all, which it was demonstrated in our previous discussion that it has not.

Socrates' dialogue with Polus

In this second part of the dialogue taken as a whole, on one level Plato allows Socrates to reach his conclusions by a series of flawed (or at least debatable) arguments, in which he trades on the ambiguities in the ethical terms involved. And Polus does not challenge any of these; he starts by derisively asserting and concludes by meekly assenting. Yet at a deeper level this sequence does enable Socrates to develop his own important and fundamental ethical and political position in stark contrast to that of Gorgias and Polus, who represent in some measure conventional beliefs. For Socrates, power and status without the knowledge to be (and do) good is no power at all, since those who wield it are mistaken about their ultimate aims ('nobody knowingly does wrong' – a famous Socratic paradox). Moreover, the argument gains in depth and conviction once the soul is brought on the scene, since, for Plato, the soul represents the essence of the individual: the pursuit of goodness leads to the health of the soul; to do evil and remain unpunished – not 'take one's medicine', to keep Socrates' analogy – leads to the reverse.

We should also note Socrates' continual presentation of his beliefs as unique and flatly contrary to those of the society in which he lives. This is reflected in contrasting views on the conduct of argument: Polus' appeal to popular consensus, and Socrates to the power of agreement reached by dialectical argument between two individuals (though what underlying conviction is to be read into Gorgias' and Polus' 'agreement' is a matter which remains open and unstated throughout the dialogue).

C: DIALOGUE WITH CALLICLES 481b6–527e7

(end of the dialogue)

C[1] 481b6–486d1

*Just as Polus was able to contain himself no longer at 461b3 (B[1] above) and jumped in to expostulate with Socrates, so here Plato repeats the dramatic pattern with Callicles. However, this more extended verbal encounter begins not with swift exchanges but with each of the speakers producing what amounts to a formal speech (*rhesis*). Socrates recalls the distinction made earlier (B[4] above) between his steady devotion to the truth of philosophy and the support in popular opinion relied on by his opponents; only this time he makes it acutely personal: the pun on *Demos*, Callicles' beloved (481d4 ff.) presents the lover as enslaved to the opinions of his beloved, the Assembly (the *demos*); this sets the tone for the much more sharply political context of the long final section of the dialogue. Callicles responds by recalling Polus' intervention in the debate with Gorgias, and in his turn accurately pinpoints Polus' key concession to Socrates (B[5] above) which had enabled Socrates to defeat him. In respecting the convention which forced him to concede that 'doing wrong' was more shameful than 'suffering wrong' (474c8), Polus was, Callicles contends, the victim of a mere debating trick, which depends on the manipulation of the concepts of 'nature' (*physis*) and 'convention' (*nomos* = 'law'). By convention it may be better to suffer than to do wrong, but in nature the opposite is the case. Callicles now broadens the debate: conventions are invented by the weak to protect themselves against the strong. By nature, Callicles argues, it is right for the stronger to rule the weaker, and in nature this is what* *happens. He concludes by reciprocating Socrates' personal attack: prolonging the study of philosophy into mature life renders individuals like Socrates and his associates bereft of the power and status to enable them to take their place in the public world of the city (*polis*).*

CALLICLES: Tell me, Chaerephon, is Socrates in earnest about this or is he joking?

CHAEREPHON: In my opinion, Callicles, he is in deadly earnest. But there's nothing like asking the man himself.

CALLICLES: By the gods, that's what I am eager to do. Tell me Socrates, are we to suppose that you are in earnest now c or joking? For if you are serious and what you say is true, won't we have human life turned upside down, and won't we be doing, apparently, the complete opposite of what we ought?

SOCRATES: O Callicles,[59] if the feelings of every human being were peculiar to himself and different from those of every other human being, instead of our possessing, for all the diversity of our experience, something in common, it would not be easy for one person to make his own situation clear to another. I say this because I have noticed that you and I now have undergone something of the same experience; we are d both lovers and for each of us his passion has a double object; I am in love with Alcibiades[60] the son of Cleinias and with philosophy, you with the *demos* of Athens and with Demos the son of Pyrilampes.[61]

Now, I observe whenever the occasion arises that for all your cleverness you are unable to contradict any assertion made by the object of your love, but shift your ground this way and that. This happens in the Assembly; if the Athenian e *demos* denies any statement made by you in a speech, you change your policy in deference to its wishes; and you behave in much the same way towards that handsome young man, the son of Pyrilampes. You are so incapable of opposing the wishes and statements of your darlings that, if surprise were expressed at the absurdity of the things which from time to time they cause you to say, you would probably answer, if

482 you wanted to be truthful, that unless your loves can be stopped from saying these things you will not stop talking as you do either.

Accept, then, that you are bound to hear a similar answer from me, and don't be surprised that I speak as I do. The only remedy is to stop *my* beloved – philosophy – from talking like this. She says, my dear friend, that which you are now hearing from me, and she is a great deal less capricious than my other love. The son of Cleinias never keeps to the same line for two minutes together, but philosophy never changes. It is her b statements which are causing your present surprise, and you yourself were there when she made them. You must then prove her wrong, as I said just now, when she asserts that wrongdoing and not being punished for wrongdoing are the worst of all evils; if you allow this to go unrefuted, Callicles, I swear by the dog which the Egyptians worship that Callicles will never be at peace with himself, but will remain at variance with himself all his life long. Yet, I think, my good fellow, that it would be better for me to have a lyre or a chorus which c I was directing in discord and out of tune, better that the mass of mankind should disagree with me and contradict me, than that I, a single individual, should be out of harmony with myself and contradict myself.[62]

CALLICLES: O Socrates, your language shows all the extravagance of a regular mob-orator; and the reason for your present harangue is that the very thing has happened to Polus that he blamed Gorgias for allowing to happen to him in his encounter with you. For Gorgias said in answer to a question from d you that if a would-be student of oratory came to him ignorant of the nature of right, he would teach it to him, and Polus declared that this answer was dictated by false shame, because a refusal would outrage the conventional notions of society, and that it was this admission which forced Gorgias into self-contradiction, which was just the thing that you love. On that occasion you thoroughly deserved Polus' mockery, in my opinion; but now Polus has suffered the same fate himself. I certainly don't admire him for agreeing with you that doing wrong is more shameful than suffering wrong; as a result of this admission he has been entangled by you in his turn and put to silence, because he was ashamed to say what he thought. The fact is, Socrates, that although you say that you are pursuing the truth, you are passing off upon your audience a vulgar, popular notion of what is fine, a notion which has its foundation in convention and not in nature.[63] e

Generally speaking, nature and convention are opposed to one another; so if from a feeling of shame a man does not dare to say what he thinks, he is forced into an inconsistency. 483 You have discovered this clever trick and make a dishonest use of it in argument; if a man speaks the language of convention, you meet him with a question framed in the language of nature; if he uses words in their natural sense, you take them in their conventional meaning. That is what has happened in this discussion of doing wrong and suffering wrong. Polus meant what is more shameful by convention, but you pursued his conventional use of the word as if he had intended its natural meaning. In nature anything that is a greater evil is also more shameful – in this case suffering wrong; but by convention doing wrong is the more shameful of the two.

The experience of suffering wrong does not happen to a b real man, but to a slave who is better off dead than alive, seeing that when he is wronged and insulted he cannot defend himself or anyone else for whom he cares. Conventions, on the other hand, are made, in my opinion, by the weaklings who form the majority of mankind. They establish them and apportion praise and blame with an eye to themselves and their own interests, and in an endeavour to frighten those who are stronger and capable of getting the upper hand they c say that taking an excess of things is shameful and wrong, and that wrongdoing consists in trying to have more than others; being inferior themselves, they are content, no doubt, if they can stand on an equal footing with their betters.

That is why by convention an attempt to have more than the majority is said to be wrong and shameful, and men call it wrongdoing; nature, on the other hand, herself demonstrates, I believe, that it is right that the better man should have more than the worse and the stronger than the weaker. d

The truth of this can be seen in a variety of examples, drawn both from the animal world and from the complex cities and nations of human beings; right is judged to be the superior ruling over the inferior and having the upper hand. By what right, for example, did Xerxes invade Greece and his father e Scythia, to take two of the countless instances[64] that one could mention? My conviction is that these actions are in accordance with nature; indeed, by Zeus, I would go so far as to say that they are in accordance with natural law, though not perhaps with the law enacted by us. Our way is to take the best and strongest among us from an early age and endeavour to mould their character as men tame lions; we subject 484 them to a course of charms and spells and enslave them by saying that men ought to be equal and that this is fine and right. But I think that if there arises a man sufficiently endowed by nature, he will shake off and break through and escape from all these trammels; he will tread underfoot our texts and spells and incantations and all our unnatural laws, and by an act of revolt reveal himself our master instead of our slave, in the full blaze of the light of natural justice. Pindar b seems to me to express the same thought as mine in the poem in which he speaks of 'Law, the king of all, men and gods alike', and goes on to say that this law 'carries things off with a high hand, making might to be right. Witness the deeds of Heracles when without paying a price . . .' or words to that effect. I do not know the poem by heart, but his meaning is c that Heracles drove off the cattle of Geryon without paying for them or receiving them as a gift, because this was natural justice, and that cattle and all other possessions of those who are weaker and inferior belong to the man who is better and superior.[65]

That is the truth of the matter, and you will realize it if from now on you abandon philosophy and turn to more important pursuits. Philosophy, Socrates, is a pleasant pastime, if one engages in it with moderation, at the right time of life; but if one pursues it further than one should it will bring ruin. However naturally gifted a person may be, if he studies philosophy beyond a suitable age he will not have acquired the necessary experience to be thought a gentleman and a person worthy of respect. d

People of this sort have no knowledge of the laws of their city, and of the language to be employed in dealings with men in private or public business, or of the human pleasures and passions; in a word, they have no idea at all how others behave. So when they are involved in any public or private matter they are as ridiculous as I imagine men of affairs to be e when they meddle with your pursuits and discussions. It comes in fact to what Euripides said:

> *Every man shines and strives for excellence*
> *In the pursuit wherein his talents lie:*
> *To this he gives the chief of all his days.*[66]

He shuns and abuses what he is weak in, and praises its 485 opposite, out of self-love and in the belief that he is thus reflecting credit upon himself.

In my opinion, however, the best course is to have some acquaintance with both practice and theory. It is a fine thing to have a tincture of philosophy, just so much as makes a person educated, and there is no disgrace in the young philosophizing. But when a man of maturer years remains devoted to this study, the thing becomes absurd, Socrates, and I have a very similar feeling about philosophers as I have b about those who stammer and play childish games. It is all very well for a child to talk and behave thus; I find it charming and delightful and quite in keeping with the tender age of a boy of free spirit; in fact, when I hear a tiny boy articulating clearly I feel distaste; it offends my ear and seems to have a slavish ring about it.[67] But whenever one hears a grown man stammering or sees him playing like a child, it is ridiculous, and he deserves a whipping for his unmanly behaviour. c

I feel just the same about students of philosophy. I admire philosophy in a young lad; it is thoroughly suitable and a mark of a free man; a lad who neglects philosophy I regard as unfree and never likely to entertain any fine or noble ambition for himself. But whenever I see an older man still d doing philosophy and refusing to abandon it, that man seems to me, Socrates, to need a whipping. As I said just now, such a person, however great his natural gifts, will never be a real man; shunning the busy life of the heart of the city and the meetings in which, as the poet says, 'men win renown',[68] he will spend the rest of his life in obscurity, whispering with three or four lads in a corner and never e saying anything independently or of sufficient importance for a free man.

Now, I am well disposed towards you, Socrates, and consequently I find myself now feeling much as Zethus felt towards Amphion in the play of Euripides that I quoted a moment ago. Indeed, I am inclined to adapt what Zethus said to his brother and to say to you: 'Socrates, you are careless of 486 what you should care for, your soul's noble nature looks like a little boy's, and the result is that you cannot contribute a word of value to the deliberations of a court, or seize upon a plausible and convincing point, or frame a bold plan in another's cause.' Do not be offended, Socrates – I am speaking out of the kindness of my heart to you – aren't you ashamed to be in this plight, which I believe you to share with all those who plunge deeper and deeper into philosophy?

As things are now, if anyone were to arrest you or one of your sort and drag you off to prison on a charge of which you were innocent, you would be quite helpless – you can be sure b of that; you would be in a daze and gape and have nothing to say, and when you got into court, however unprincipled a rascal the prosecutor might be, you would be condemned to death, if he chose to ask for the death penalty.[69]

But what kind of wisdom can we call it, Socrates, this art that 'takes a man of talent and spoils his gifts', so that he cannot defend himself or another from mortal danger, but c lets his enemies rob him of all his goods, and lives to all intents and purposes the life of an outlaw in his own city? A man like that, if you will pardon a rather blunt expression, can be slapped on the face with complete impunity.

Take my advice then, my good friend; 'abandon argument, practise the accomplishments of active life', which will give you the reputation of a prudent man. 'Leave others to split hairs' of what I don't know whether to call folly or nonsense; 'their only outcome is that you will inhabit a barren house.'[70] Take for your models not the men who spend their time on these petty quibbles, but those who have a livelihood and reputation and many other good things. d

C[2] 486d2–488b1

A short interlude which again (see A[5] and B[4] above) examines the nature of the discussion. Socrates replies to Callicles' attack by complimenting him on his exceptional understanding, goodwill and frankness – a 'touchstone' which will, Socrates maintains, be adequate to test the truth of whatever conclusions they will both come to together. However, Callicles does not live up to Socrates' compliments; despite Callicles' promising start, he ultimately proves as deficient in understanding and frankness as Gorgias and Polus were. His lack of goodwill is indicated by the fact that, unlike them, he does not concede when beaten in argument.

SOCRATES: If my soul were made of gold, Callicles, can you not imagine how happy I should be to light upon one of those touchstones by which gold is tested? I should like it to be of the best possible kind, so that if, when I tried the condition of my soul against it, and it agreed that my soul was well cared for, I could be perfectly confident of being in a good state and in need of no further test.

CALLICLES: What is the point of this, Socrates? e

SOCRATES: I will tell you. I believe that in meeting you I have hit upon just such a lucky find.

CALLICLES: What do you mean?

SOCRATES: I am quite sure that if *you* agree with me about anything of which I am convinced in my soul, we shall have there the actual truth. I have noticed that anyone who is to make an adequate test as to whether a soul is living well or 487 the reverse must have three qualities, all of which you possess:

understanding, goodwill and readiness to be perfectly frank. I encounter many people who are not qualified to put me to the test because they are not wise like you; others are wise but unwilling to tell me the truth because they have not the same regard for me as you; and our two guests here, Gorgias b and Polus, though they are well disposed towards me as well as wise, are nevertheless somewhat lacking in frankness and more hampered by inhibitions than they ought to be. It is obvious that these inhibitions extend so far that each of them has been reduced by false shame to contradict himself before a large audience and on extremely important matters.

You, however, possess all those qualities which the others lack; you have had a sound education, as many Athenians would declare, and you are well disposed towards me. If you ask what evidence I have of this, Callicles, I will tell you. I c know that you have been a partner in philosophical discussion with Tisander of Aphidna, Andron the son of Androtion, and Nausicydes of Cholargeis,[71] and I once overheard the four of you debating how far one ought to pursue philosophy. I know that the prevailing view was that one should not aim at any very exact study of it and you warned one another to be d careful, for fear of finding, when it was too late, that you had ruined yourselves by over-education. So when I hear from you now the same advice as you gave to your most intimate friends, I have sufficient proof that you sincerely wish me well. As for your being the sort of man who speaks his mind without any sort of inhibition, you say it yourself and the speech which you have just made is in accord.

e Clearly, then, this is how matters stand at present. Any point on which you agree with me we can regard on both sides as adequately tested; there will be no need to apply any other touchstone, since you will never acquiesce from lack of wisdom or excess of false shame or from any desire to deceive me, as by your own account, you are my friend. So then it will be no exaggeration to say that agreement between us is bound to result in truth.

In spite of your reproaches, Callicles, there can be no finer 488 subject for discussion than the question what a man should be like and what occupation he should engage in and how far he should pursue it, both in earlier and later life. If anything in the conduct of my life is amiss, be sure that this arises from ignorance on my part, not from wilfulness; so do not abandon the attempt to instruct me, which you have begun, but give me a thorough demonstration of what occupation I ought to follow and how I can best embark on it. And if hereafter you find that I fail to put into practice anything to which I now give my assent, call me a complete idiot and never waste your b advice on such a good-for-nothing again.

The belief, assumed here by Socrates, that conclusions mutually agreed on by able and sincere debaters 'are bound to result in truth' raises fundamental questions about the adequacy of the elenchus *as an argumentative structure for arriving at truth rather than mere consistency of belief (see the Introduction, 'Structure and argument').*

C[3] 488b2–491d3

Socrates does not immediately defend himself from Callicles' attack, but goes to work on his claim by attempting to get him to clarify what he meant by 'stronger' when he asserted that 'it is right that the better man should have more than the worse and the stronger than the weaker' (483d1–2). In Plato's dialogues, Socrates' requests for clarification typically aim to uncover inconsistencies in his opponents' positions; here, in the initial argument, he actually shows that Callicles' assertion implies the exact opposite of what he claims: since the majority (by virtue of number) is stronger than the individual, then the laws imposed by the majority (the stronger) are better, and the majority believe that it is more shameful to do than to suffer wrong; so this is true by nature as well as by convention. To avoid formally conceding this, Callicles resorts to abuse and then shifts his ground: he accepts Socrates' suggestion that he might mean that the 'better' and 'stronger' are the 'more intelligent' (489e8). Socrates then goes to work on this; the wiser man, by analogy with other 'experts' (e.g. doctors, weavers, shoemakers, farmers) should not, by virtue of being wise, take a larger share of goods than others. Callicles then shifts position yet again: to intelligence he adds bravery. By virtue of their superior intelligence and courage, outstanding individuals should rule and have more than others.

SOCRATES: Go back to the beginning and tell me again what you and Pindar mean by natural right. Am I mistaken in thinking that according to you right consists in the stronger taking the property of the weaker by force and the better ruling the worse and the nobler having more than the person of lesser worth?

CALLICLES: No; that is what I said then and what I still maintain.

SOCRATES: But do you mean that 'better' and 'stronger' are
c the same? I couldn't make out just what you meant on this point. Do you mean by 'stronger' those who have greater physical strength, and must the weaker obey the stronger, as you seemed to imply when you spoke of big cities attacking small ones in accordance with natural right, because they are stronger and physically more powerful, as if 'more powerful' and 'stronger' and 'better' were synonymous terms? Is it possible to be better, but at the same time less powerful and weaker, and stronger, but also more vicious? Or are 'better'
d and 'stronger' to be defined as the same? This is the point on which I want a clear definition; are 'stronger' and 'better' and 'more powerful' synonymous or not?

CALLICLES: I tell you quite explicitly that they are synonymous.

SOCRATES: Now, are not the mass of people naturally stronger than the individual? And these are the people, as you were saying just now, who impose their laws upon the individual.

CALLICLES: Of course.

SOCRATES: Then the laws imposed by the majority are laws imposed by the stronger.

CALLICLES: Certainly.

e SOCRATES: And therefore by the better ? The stronger are also the better by your account, I think.

CALLICLES: Yes.

SOCRATES: Then since they are stronger, the laws which they establish are by nature good?

CALLICLES: I agree.

SOCRATES: But is it not the belief of the majority, as you were saying yourself just now, that equality is right and that it is a more shameful thing to do wrong than to suffer wrong? Answer yes or no, and take care that you in your turn are not 489 betrayed by a feeling of shame. Do the majority believe or do they not that equality, not inequality, is right and that it is more shameful to do wrong than to suffer wrong? Don't grudge me an answer to this question, Callicles. If you agree with me, let me hear the point established on your authority, the authority of a man well able to decide the matter.

CALLICLES: Very well, that is the belief of the masses.

SOCRATES: Then the belief that it is more shameful to do wrong than to suffer wrong and that equality is right appears to be founded in nature as well as in convention. It looks as if what b you said earlier was not true, and you were in error when you said that convention and nature were opposites, and accused me of making a dishonest use of this knowledge in argument by taking in a conventional sense words intended by the speaker in a natural sense, and vice versa.

CALLICLES: There is no end to the rubbish this fellow talks. Tell me, Socrates, aren't you ashamed at your age of laying these verbal traps[72] and counting it a godsend if a man makes a slip of the tongue? Do you really suppose that by 'stronger' c I mean anything but 'better'? Haven't I already told you that they are the same? Do you take me to mean that, if you sweep together a heap of slaves and riff-raff useful only perhaps for their brawn, and they say this or that, what they say is to have the force of the law?

SOCRATES: Ah! my clever friend, is that the line you take?

CALLICLES: Certainly it is.

SOCRATES: Well, my fine fellow, I guessed some time ago d that that or something like it was what you understood by 'stronger' and my repeating the question arises from my eagerness to grasp your precise meaning. Of course you don't believe that two men are better than one or your slaves better than you, simply because they are physically more powerful. Tell me again from the start what you mean by 'better' since you don't mean 'more powerful'. And I must ask you, my friend, to be a little milder in your style of teaching; otherwise I shall run away from your school.

e CALLICLES: You are being ironic Socrates.[73]

SOCRATES: No, Callicles, I am not; I swear it by Zethus, whose person you borrowed just now for much irony at my expense. Come now, tell me whom you mean by 'better' men.

CALLICLES: I mean those who are nobler.

SOCRATES: Then don't you see that you too are uttering mere words and clarifying nothing?[74] Tell me, do you mean by 'better' and 'stronger' those who are more intelligent, or something else?

CALLICLES: That is exactly what I do mean, most emphatically.

490 SOCRATES: Then on your theory it must often happen that one wise man is stronger than ten thousand fools, and that he ought to rule over them as subjects and have the lion's share of everything. That is what you seem to mean – there is no verbal trap here, I assure you – if one man is stronger than ten thousand.

CALLICLES: That is exactly what I do mean. My belief is that natural right consists in the better and wiser man ruling over his inferiors and having the lion's share.

b SOCRATES: Stop there one moment. What exactly do you mean this time? Suppose a number of us were collected in the same spot, as we are now, with plenty of food and drink between us, a heterogeneous crowd of strong and weak together, but containing one man wiser than the rest of us about such matters because he is a doctor. And suppose that this man, as is quite likely, were physically more powerful than some but less powerful than other members of the crowd. Should we say that for the present purpose the doctor, being wiser than we are, is also better and stronger?

CALLICLES: Certainly.

c SOCRATES: Is he then to have more of the food than we because he is better, or is his authority over us to be shown by his being in control of the distribution? If he is not to suffer for it, he should not appropriate the largest ration for his personal consumption; he ought to have more than some and less than others, and if he happens to be the greatest invalid of the party, the best man should get the smallest share. Isn't that how it ought to be, Callicles?

CALLICLES: You talk of food and drink and doctors and nonsense of that sort. That is not what I am referring to. d

SOCRATES: Then do you maintain that the wiser man is also the better? Yes or no.

CALLICLES: Yes.

SOCRATES: But should the better man not have the larger share?

CALLICLES: Yes, but not of food and drink.

SOCRATES: Very well; perhaps you mean of clothes, and the best weaver ought to have the biggest coat, and go about the town in more and finer clothes than other people.

CALLICLES: Clothes now!

SOCRATES: As for shoes, obviously the man who is best and wisest about them will have the advantage there; the shoe- e maker will, I suppose, walk about in the largest shoes and have the greatest number of them.

CALLICLES: Shoes indeed! You keep up this nonsense!

SOCRATES: If you don't mean that sort of thing, perhaps you mean, for example, that a farmer, who is intelligent and a fine fellow where land is concerned, should have a larger share of seed than other people, and use the greatest possible quantity of seed on his own farm.

CALLICLES: Always the same old language, Socrates.

SOCRATES: Yes, Callicles, and on the same subjects.

CALLICLES: By the gods, you simply never stop talking of 491 cobblers and fullers and cooks and doctors; as if our argument were concerned with them!

SOCRATES: Then kindly tell me in what sphere a man must show his greater strength and intelligence in order to establish a right to more than others. Or are you going to turn down my suggestions, and at the same time make none of your own?

CALLICLES: I have told you already what I mean. First of all, when I speak of 'stronger' I don't mean cobblers or cooks; I mean people with the intelligence to know how the city's b affairs should be handled, and not only intelligence but courage; people who have the ability to carry out their ideas, and who will not give up from faintness of heart.

SOCRATES: Do you notice, my excellent Callicles, how you and I find fault with one another for quite different reasons? You blame me for constantly using the same language, while I, on the contrary, criticize you for never keeping to the same line about the same subject. At one moment you defined the c better and stronger as the more powerful, next as the more intelligent, and now you come out with yet another idea: you say that the better and stronger are a braver sort of people. Tell us my good friend, and be done with it, what you mean by the better and stronger and how they differ from other people.

CALLICLES: I have told you that I mean people who are intelligent in the city's affairs and have courage. They are the people d who ought to rule cities, and right consists in the rulers having more than the ruled.

In presenting Callicles' views here, Plato is reflecting, albeit in extreme form, the moral and social attitudes (the striving for arete *= 'excellence') of the type of upper-class young Athenian Callicles represents. But his beliefs are vulnerable to Socrates' probing; he is forced by Socrates to distinguish between 'stronger' and 'better', thus revealing that his individualistic 'superiority' in Athenian society depends on the acquiescence, even the acclaim, of the (stronger) majority, So, Callicles' shifts of position here reflect the underlying inconsistency of his anti-democratic attitudes (on Callicles' contradictory positions, see especially Woolf 2000).*

It is important to note, however, that Socrates is not, in his suggestion that the majority are 'stronger' (488d5 ff.), supporting conventional democratic values. This line of argument is temporarily convenient to refute Callicles, but Plato was in essence as much an authoritarian as Callicles, although of a very different sort. The introduction of the 'expert' craftsman, which was a feature of the argument with Gorgias (A[6] above), and which here Callicles ridicules as a Socratic stock-in-trade ('you simply never stop talking of cobblers and fullers and cooks and doctors', 491a1–2), foreshadows the introduction of what Plato envisages as the real politician and ruler, the expert, who has not his own best interests at heart but those of the ruled.

C[4] 491d4–495c2

491d4 ff. represents a sharp change of tack by Socrates; in the Polus discussion he questioned whether the person with unlimited power is 'happy' (eudaimon, *see B[3] commentary above) in the sense of knowing what is good (for him). Callicles has already rejected that line of argument (C[1]) by accepting the end-point, 'good' or 'happiness', but giving it a new content – power over others. Here Socrates turns his attention to the internal aspect of absolute power, the indulgence of unlimited appetites: won't the moderate individual be happier than the person who takes things to excess? The latter must continually seek to fill himself up with new pleasures as the old run away; he will be insatiable, whereas the temperate person is content with what he has. Socrates introduces into the discussion the important idea of 'moderation' or 'self-control' (*sophrosune*), one of the four cardinal virtues in Greek thought, which, he claims, is more likely to lead to 'happiness' (*eudaimonia*); Callicles, on the other hand, speaks of 'pleasure' (*hedone*), which he implicitly identifies with happiness and the good (see 494a3 and 7). Rather than aim at direct refutation, Socrates leads Callicles into the vulgar consequences of his position – satisfaction of any desire, however base, must be good. Callicles is duly shocked and succumbs to shame, but still maintains this position to avoid the accusation of inconsistency. Socrates' arguments here are designed more to provoke Callicles' disgusted reactions (which are conventional for all his radical views) than to get to the heart of the issue. The proposition that pleasure and happiness are identical has not yet been refuted.*

SOCRATES: But what of themselves, my friend? Rulers or ruled there?[75]

CALLICLES: What do you mean?

SOCRATES: I mean each man being master of himself. Or is there no need for self-mastery as long as one is master of others?

CALLICLES: What do you mean by self-mastery?

SOCRATES: Nothing fancy. I use the word simply in the popular sense, of being moderate and in control of oneself and master e of one's own passions and appetites.

CALLICLES: What a funny fellow you are, Socrates. The people who you call moderate are the half-witted.

SOCRATES: How so? Anybody can see that I don't mean that.

CALLICLES: Oh! but you do, Socrates. For how can a man be happy who is in subjection to anyone whoever? I tell you frankly that what is fine and right by nature consists in this: that the man who is going to live as a man ought should 492 encourage his appetites to be as strong as possible instead of repressing them, and be able by means of his courage and intelligence to satisfy them in all their intensity by providing them with whatever they happen to desire.

For the majority, I believe, this is an impossible ideal; that is why, in an endeavour to conceal their own weakness, they blame the minority whom they are ashamed of not being able to imitate, and maintain that excess is a disgraceful thing. As I said before,[76] they try to make slaves of those who are better by nature, and because through their own lack of manliness they are unable to satisfy their passions, they praise moderation and righteousness. To those who are either the sons of b kings to begin with or able by their own qualities to win office or absolute rule or sovereignty, what could in truth be more disgraceful or worse than moderation and justice, which involves their voluntary subjection to the conventions and standards and criticism of the majority, when they might enjoy good things without interference from anybody? How can they fail to be wretched when they are prevented by c your fine righteousness and moderation from favouring their friends at the expense of their enemies, even when they are rulers in their own city?

The truth, Socrates, which you profess to be in search of, is in fact this: luxury and excess and licence, provided that they can obtain sufficient backing, are virtue and happiness;[77] all the rest is mere pretence, man-made rules contrary to nature, worthless cant.

SOCRATES: Your frank development of your position, Callicles, certainly does not lack spirit. You set out plainly in the light of day opinions which other people think but are not willing to express. Don't weaken at all, I beseech you, so that we may come to a clear conclusion how life should be lived. And tell me this. You maintain, do you not, that if a man is to be what he ought he should not repress his appetites but let them grow as strong as possible and satisfy them by any means in his power, and that such behaviour is virtue? d e

CALLICLES: Yes, that's what I say.

SOCRATES: Then the view that those who have no wants are happy is wrong?

CALLICLES: Of course; at that rate stones and corpses would be supremely happy.

SOCRATES: Nevertheless even the life which you describe is strange. I should not wonder if Euripides may not be right when he says:

Who knows if life be death or death be life?[78]

and if perhaps it may not be we who are in fact dead. This is a view that I have heard before now from one of the sages, that we in our present condition are dead. Our body is the tomb in which we are buried,[79] and the part of the soul containing our appetites is liable to be seduced and carried in contrary directions. This same part, because of its instability and readiness to be influenced, a witty man – Sicilian perhaps or Italian[80] – has by a play upon words allegorically called a pitcher. In the same vein he labels fools 'uninitiated', and that part of their soul which contains the appetites, which 493 b is intemperate and, as it were, the reverse of watertight, he represents as a pitcher with holes in it, because it cannot be filled up.[81] Thus in direct opposition to you, Callicles, this man maintains that of all the inhabitants of Hades – meaning by Hades the invisible world[82] – the uninitiated are the most wretched, being engaged in pouring water into a leaky pitcher c out of an equally leaky sieve.[83] The sieve, according to my informant, he uses as an image of the soul, and his motive for comparing the souls of fools to sieves is that they are leaky and unable to retain their contents on account of their fickle and forgetful nature. This comparison is, no doubt, a bit grotesque, but it demonstrates the point which I want to prove to you, to persuade you, if I can, to change your mind, and, instead of a life of intemperate craving which can never be satisfied, to choose an ordered life which is content with whatever comes to hand and asks no more.

d Does what I say influence you at all towards a conviction that the temperate are happier than the intemperate, or will any number of such stories fail to convert you?

CALLICLES: That's nearer the truth, Socrates.

SOCRATES: Well, let me produce another simile from the same school as the first. Suppose that the two lives, the temperate and the intemperate, are typified by two men, each of whom has a number of casks. The casks of the first are sound and e full, one of wine, one of honey, one of milk, and so on, but the supply of each of these commodities is scanty and he can procure them only with very great difficulty. This man, when once he has filled his casks, will not need to draw in any more or give himself any further concern about it; as far as this matter goes his mind will be at rest. Now take the second man. He, like the first, can obtain a supply, though only with difficulty; but his vessels are leaky and rotten, so that if he is 494 to avoid the extremity of privation he must be perpetually filling them, day and night. If such is the condition of each of the two lives, can you say that the life of the intemperate man is happier than the life of the temperate? Am I making any progress towards making you admit that the temperate life is better than the intemperate, or not?

CALLICLES: No, Socrates, you are not. The man who has filled his casks no longer has any pleasure left. It is just as I said a moment ago; once his casks are filled he lives like a stone, with no more pleasure and pain. But the pleasure of life b consists precisely in this, that there should be as much flowing in as possible.

SOCRATES: But if much is to run in, much must necessarily flow out, and there must be large holes for it to escape by.

CALLICLES: Certainly.

SOCRATES: Then, the life which you are describing, so far from being that of a stone or a corpse, is that of a Charadrios, a greedy and messy bird.[84] Tell me now; are you speaking of such things as being hungry and eating when one is hungry?

CALLICLES: Yes.

SOCRATES: And of being thirsty and drinking when one is c thirsty?

CALLICLES: Certainly, and of having all the other appetites and being able to satisfy them with enjoyment. That is the happy life.

SOCRATES: Excellent, my friend. Only you must stick to your point and not give way out of shame. No more must I, for that matter, it seems. Tell me first of all, can a man who itches and wants to scratch and whose opportunities of scratching are unbounded be said to lead a happy life continually scratching?

CALLICLES: How strange you are, Socrates, and how d thoroughly vulgar.

SOCRATES: That, Callicles, is why I shocked Polus and Gorgias and made them feel shame. But you are a brave man, and will never give way to such emotions. Just answer me.

CALLICLES: Then I say that even the man who scratches would live a pleasant life.

SOCRATES: And if pleasant then happy?

CALLICLES: Of course.

SOCRATES: But if it was only his head he scratches, or . . . Must e I go on with my questions? Consider what answer you will make, Callicles, if you are asked all the questions which are linked to this. To bring the matter to a head, take the life of a catamite: isn't that dreadful and shameful and wretched? Or will you dare to say that such people are happy provided that they have an abundant supply of what they want?

CALLICLES: Aren't you ashamed to introduce such subjects into the discussion, Socrates?

SOCRATES: Who is responsible for their introduction, my noble friend? I or the person who maintains without qualification that those who feel enjoyment of whatever kind are happy, and who does not distinguish between good and bad pleas- 495 ures? Tell me once more, do you declare that pleasure is identical with good, or are there some pleasures which are not good?

CALLICLES: To say that they are different would involve me in an inconsistency. I declare that they are identical.

SOCRATES: If you say what you do not think, Callicles, you are destroying the force of your first speech, and I can no longer accept you as a satisfactory ally in my attempt to discover the truth.

b CALLICLES: But you are doing just the same, Socrates.

SOCRATES: If I do that, I am wrong and so are you. Can it be, my good friend, that good is not identical with enjoyment of whatever kind? Otherwise many shameful consequences will ensue besides those at which I have just hinted.

CALLICLES: That is what *you* think, Socrates.

SOCRATES: Do you really persist, Callicles, in what you affirm?

CALLICLES: Yes, I do.

c SOCRATES: Shall we then continue the argument on the assumption that you are serious?

CALLICLES: By all means.

C[5] 495c3–500a6

Socrates proceeds to deploy two arguments to show that Callicles is wrong and that pleasure and good cannot be identical: 1. 495c3–497d8 (a) good and happiness cannot be present in the same thing in the same place and at the same time as evil and misery, while pleasure and pain can (for example, in the case of the satisfaction of hunger and thirst); (b) therefore having pleasure and pain is not the same as experiencing good and evil. 2. *497d8–499b3 (a) fools and the intelligent have (more or less) equal capacity for feeling pleasure and pain; (b) cowards have (more or less) the same capacity as the brave for feeling joy and pain; (c) the wise are brave and good, fools and cowards bad; (d) thus the bad feel joy and pain about as much as the good (from (a)–(c)); (e) he who is good feels joy, he who is bad feels pain; (f) therefore, if pleasure and good are identical, the bad man is just as good and bad as the good man, and vice versa (i.e. the bad man is no worse than the good man).*

In the face of this reductio ad absurdum, *Callicles abruptly abandons his position and concedes (though he does not present it as a concession) that there are better and worse pleasures. Having expressed mock surprise at Callicles' change of tack, Socrates develops a 'new' position, which enables him to return to the line of argument he was pursuing with Polus (B[2] above): 'all actions should be performed as a means to the good'. And the final vital concession – that such calculations are the job of the expert – reaches back to the discussion with Gorgias and Polus of experts and genuine and pseudo arts in A[6] and B[1].*

SOCRATES: Very well then; if that is your decision, solve this problem. You recognize the existence of something called knowledge, I presume?

CALLICLES: Yes.

SOCRATES: You were speaking just now, were you not, of courage existing together with knowledge?

CALLICLES: I was.

SOCRATES: Meaning, I suppose, that courage and knowledge are two different things.

CALLICLES: Very different.

SOCRATES: Now then; would you call pleasure and knowledge the same or different?

CALLICLES: Different, of course; you are so clever! d

SOCRATES: And courage different from pleasure?

CALLICLES: Of course.

SOCRATES: We must make a note of this: 'Callicles of Archarnae declared that pleasure and good are the same, but knowledge and courage are different from one another and different from good.'

CALLICLES: 'But Socrates of Alopece[85] does not agree with him', or does he?

e SOCRATES: He does not. Nor, I think, will Callicles, when he has examined himself properly. Tell me, do you not think that the fortunate are in the opposite state to the unfortunate?

CALLICLES: Yes.

SOCRATES: Then, if these states are opposite, is not the same true of them as health and sickness? A person, of course, is never both well and sick at the same time, and doesn't stop being well and sick at the same time.

CALLICLES: What do you mean?

SOCRATES: For instance, take any part of the body you like by
496 itself: suppose a man has a malady of the eyes, what is called ophthalmia.

CALLICLES: Very well.

SOCRATES: He does not, I presume, enjoy health in his eyes at the same time?

CALLICLES: Not at all.

SOCRATES: Now, what happens when he loses his ophthalmia? Does he at that moment lose health in his eyes, so that he ends by losing both together?

CALLICLES: Certainly not.

b SOCRATES: Such a conclusion would be illogical as well as surprising, wouldn't it?

CALLICLES: It would indeed.

SOCRATES: The truth is, I imagine, that he acquires and loses each condition by turns.

CALLICLES: I agree.

SOCRATES: Is the same true of strength and weakness?

CALLICLES: Yes.

SOCRATES: And of quickness and slowness?

CALLICLES: Of course.

SOCRATES: Now, take good and happiness and their opposites,

evil and misery; are both of these acquired by turns and lost by turns?

CALLICLES: Unquestionably.

SOCRATES: Then, if we find any pair of opposites that a man loses together and possesses together, they will not be good and evil. Are we agreed about this? Think well before you answer. c

CALLICLES: I agree most emphatically.

SOCRATES: Go back now to what we agreed before. You spoke of hunger; did you mean that it was pleasant or painful? I mean just hunger by itself.

CALLICLES: I should call that painful; but to eat when one is hungry is pleasant. d

SOCRATES: I understand. Still, hunger in itself is painful, is it not?

CALLICLES: Yes.

SOCRATES: And thirst also?

CALLICLES: Certainly.

SOCRATES: Shall I go on with further questions, or do you agree that every state of want and desire is painful?

CALLICLES: You need not labour the point. I agree.

SOCRATES: Very well. But drinking when one is thirsty you would call pleasant, wouldn't you?

CALLICLES: Yes.

SOCRATES: And drinking is the satisfaction of the want and a pleasure? e

CALLICLES: Yes.

SOCRATES: So it is in connection with drinking that you speak of enjoyment?

CALLICLES: Certainly.

SOCRATES: When one is thirsty?

CALLICLES: Yes.

SOCRATES: And therefore in pain?

CALLICLES: Yes.

SOCRATES: So, do you see what follows? When you speak of someone drinking when thirsty you imply the experience of enjoyment and pain together. Can you say that these sensations don't occur together at the same time and in the same part of something which you may equally well, I think, call body or soul? Is this true or not?

CALLICLES: Quite true.

SOCRATES: Yet you say that it is impossible to be fortunate and unfortunate at the same time.

CALLICLES: I do.

497 SOCRATES: But you have agreed that it is possible to feel enjoyment when one is in pain.

CALLICLES: So it appears.

SOCRATES: Then enjoyment is not the same as good fortune nor pain as bad fortune, so that pleasure turns out to be different from good.

CALLICLES: I don't understand your quibbles, Socrates.

SOCRATES: Oh yes, you do, Callicles; only it suits you to feign ignorance. Just carry the argument a little further.

CALLICLES: What is the point of continuing this nonsense?

SOCRATES: So that you can see how clever you are, when you b admonish me. Is it not true that at the moment when each of us ceases to feel thirst, he ceases also to feel the pleasure of drinking?

CALLICLES: I don't know what you mean.

GORGIAS: Oh no, Callicles; answer to please *us* as well as Socrates, so that the argument can be brought to an end.

CALLICLES: But Socrates is always the same, Gorgias. He catches one out by such trivial and worthless questions.

GORGIAS: What does that matter to you? It is not your reputation which is at stake, Callicles.[86] Allow Socrates to conduct the argument in his own way.

c CALLICLES: Well, go on with your petty little questions, since Gorgias will have it so.

SOCRATES: You're a happy man, Callicles, to have been initiated into the Greater Mysteries before the Lesser; I didn't think that it was allowed.[87] Go on where you left off, and tell me whether we don't all finish with thirst and pleasure at the same time.

CALLICLES: Yes, we do.

SOCRATES: And the same with hunger and the other appetites?

Does not the pleasure of satisfying them cease at the same moment as the desire?

CALLICLES: True.

SOCRATES: Then pains and pleasures come to an end together? d

CALLICLES: Yes.

SOCRATES: But, as you agreed, good and evil do not come to an end together. Or do you wish now to disagree?

CALLICLES: By no means. So what?

SOCRATES: This, my friend – that good is not identical with pleasure nor evil with pain. The one pair of contraries comes to an end together and the other does not, because they are different. How then can pleasure possibly be the same as good, or pain as evil? Look at the matter in another way if you like: the conclusion will still, I think, be at variance with yours. When you call people good, you imply, do you not, e the presence of good in them, in the same way as you call those in whom beauty is present beautiful?

CALLICLES: Yes.

SOCRATES: Well, do you call fools and cowards good? You didn't just now; you reserved the term for the brave and intelligent. They are the people you call good, aren't they?

CALLICLES: Certainly.

SOCRATES: Well, have you ever seen a foolish child enjoying itself?

CALLICLES: Yes.

SOCRATES: And for that matter a foolish man enjoying himself?

CALLICLES: I suppose so. But what is the point of this?

SOCRATES: Nothing; just answer. 498

CALLICLES: Yes, then.

SOCRATES: Have you seen an intelligent man feeling pain or pleasure?

CALLICLES: Yes.

SOCRATES: Well, which group feels greater pain or pleasure, the fools or the wise men?

CALLICLES: I don't know that there is much in it.

SOCRATES: That is enough for my purpose. Now, have you seen a coward in war?

CALLICLES: Of course.

SOCRATES: And when the enemy retreated, which did you think felt greater joy, the cowards or the brave men?

CALLICLES: Greater joy? Both, as far as I could see, or perhaps the cowards felt more; anyhow the difference was trifling.

b SOCRATES: It makes no difference. At any rate cowards feel joy as well as the brave?

CALLICLES: Undoubtedly.

SOCRATES: And fools too, it seems.

CALLICLES: Yes.

SOCRATES: But when the enemy advances, is pain confined to cowards, or do the brave feel it too?

CALLICLES: Both feel it.

SOCRATES: Equally?

CALLICLES: Perhaps cowards feel it more.

SOCRATES: And don't they feel greater joy when the enemy retreats?

CALLICLES: Perhaps.

SOCRATES: Then, by your account pain and joy are felt in practically the same degree by fools and wise men, cowards and the brave, but if anything more keenly by cowards than c by brave men?

CALLICLES: Yes.

SOCRATES: Yet the wise and brave are good, and the cowards and fools bad?

CALLICLES: Yes.

SOCRATES: Then good and bad feel joy and pain in about the same degree?

CALLICLES: Yes.

SOCRATES: In that case are we to conclude that there is very little to choose in goodness and badness between the good and the bad, or even that the bad are somewhat better than the good?

d CALLICLES: By Zeus, I don't know what you mean.

SOCRATES: Don't you know that you are maintaining that the good owe their goodness to the presence in them of good, and the bad their badness to the presence of evil, and that good is identical with pleasure and evil with pain?

CALLICLES: Yes.

SOCRATES: Doesn't the sensation of joy involve the presence of good, that is pleasure, in those who experience it?

CALLICLES: Of course.

SOCRATES: Then since good is present in them, those who feel joy are good?

CALLICLES: Yes.

SOCRATES: Again, is not evil, that is pain, present in those who suffer pain?

CALLICLES: It is.

SOCRATES: And you say that the bad owe their badness to the presence of evil in them. Or do you no longer say that? e

CALLICLES: No, I say it.

SOCRATES: Then whoever feels joy is good and whoever feels pain is bad?

CALLICLES: Certainly.

SOCRATES: And people are more or less or equally good or bad just as their experience of joy or pain is more or less or equally intense?

CALLICLES: Yes.

SOCRATES: You say, I think, that joy and pain are felt in almost equal degree by wise men and fools, cowards and brave men, or possibly somewhat more keenly by cowards?

CALLICLES: Yes.

SOCRATES: Now, give me your help in drawing the conclusion that emerges from what we have agreed. 'What is worth saying is worth saying (and investigating) twice or thrice,' they say. We affirm that a wise and brave man is good, don't we? 499

CALLICLES: Yes.

SOCRATES: And a fool and a coward bad?

CALLICLES: Certainly.

SOCRATES: But a man who feels joy is good?

CALLICLES: Yes.

SOCRATES: And a man who feels pain bad?

CALLICLES: Inevitably.

SOCRATES: And the good and bad feel pain and joy alike, but the bad perhaps more keenly?

CALLICLES: Yes.

SOCRATES: Then the bad man is as good and as bad as the
b good, or perhaps rather better. Isn't this the conclusion that follows from what we agreed before, if one begins by equating pleasure and good? Is there any escape from it Callicles?

CALLICLES: I've been listening to you and expressing agreement for a long time, Socrates, with the thought in my mind all along that if one gives in to you on any point, even in jest, you seize on the admission triumphantly with all the eagerness of an adolescent. As if you didn't know that, like everybody else, I distinguish between better and worse pleasures.

c SOCRATES: Oh, oh, Callicles, what a rogue you are! You are treating me like a child, changing your ground from moment to moment, to mislead me. And yet, when we began I never supposed that you would wilfully mislead me, because I thought that you were my friend. But now it appears that I was mistaken in you, and I suppose that I must make the best of it, as the saying goes, and do what I can with what you choose to give me. What you are now saying, apparently, is that somc pleasures are good and some bad. Is that right?

d CALLICLES: Yes.

SOCRATES: Are good pleasures those which bring benefit and bad pleasures those which bring harm?

CALLICLES: Of course.

SOCRATES: And the beneficial are those which produce some good result, and the harmful those which produce the reverse?

CALLICLES: Yes.

SOCRATES: Now, do you mean the sort of pleasures we were speaking of before, the physical pleasures of eating and drinking, for example? Are we to regard those which produce bodily health or strength or some other physical excellence as good and those which have the opposite effect as bad?

CALLICLES: Certainly.

e SOCRATES: And does the same apply to pains? Are some good and some bad?

CALLICLES: Naturally.

SOCRATES: Then we should choose and follow the good of both kinds, pains as well as pleasures?

CALLICLES: By all means.

SOCRATES: And reject the bad?

CALLICLES: Obviously.

SOCRATES: If you remember, Polus and I agreed that all actions should be performed as a means to the good.[88] Do you also agree with this, that good is the object of all actions, and that all that we do should be a means to the good, and not vice versa? Are you prepared to add your vote to our two? 500

CALLICLES: Yes, I am.

SOCRATES: Then it follows that we should pursue pleasure among other things as a means to good, and not good as a means to pleasure.

CALLICLES: Certainly.

SOCRATES: Can *anybody* distinguish between good and bad pleasures, or does it need an expert in each case?

CALLICLES: It needs an expert.

Socrates' two arguments appear to be constructed in some respects with the sophistic techniques Plato so despises: 1. in particular rests on the rather shaky foundation of the assumption that pain and pleasure are simultaneously *present in the satisfying of appetites like hunger (Plato elsewhere suggests that pleasure and pain are inextricably connected rather than simultaneous (*Phaedo *60b4) or pleasure can be 'unmixed', i.e. totally unassociated with any previous discomfort, as in smell or intellectual pleasures (e.g.* Philebus *51a ff.)). One has some sympathy here with Callicles' protest about Socrates' 'petty little questions' (497c1; on these arguments, see Santas 1979, pp. 267 ff.; Kahn 1983, p. 109; Beversluis 2000, p. 356). However, as in the case of the argument against Polus in B[5] above, which it slightly resembles, Socrates' proofs, even if shaky in themselves, are enough to demonstrate the untenable nature of Callicles' position on the identity of pleasure and good. The basic incoherence of Callicles' advocacy of courage and intelligence side by side with his ideal of unlimited satisfaction of desire is blatant: the former require restraint which the latter denies; and this fundamental weakness in Callicles' position is independent of the validity of Socrates' arguments here. Callicles' abrupt abandonment of his position and his transparent attempt to* *disguise the fact with personal abuse of Socrates is consistent with Plato's presentation of his character throughout this part of* Gorgias.

C[6] 500a7–505b12

Now begins the major second part of the argument with Callicles. So far the discussion has been concerned with refuting Callicles' identification of good with pleasure. In the second half, Socrates broadens the debate to encompass the question of 'how a person should live' (500c3–4). The question of the value of the 'two lives' – that of the conventional politician and that of the philosopher – gradually assumes a central position in the discussion. Socrates also returns to a theme temporarily abandoned in the dialogue with Polus: the contrast between genuine and spurious arts (B[1] above), which Socrates now relates to the activities of the political orator; all political leaders aim at the satisfaction of the desires of the masses ('pandering' to them, e.g. 503a6), and not at what is best for their souls; what is best for the soul is a state of order and proportion, and the genuine politician will have as his aim the cultivation of these qualities in the souls of the citizens in his charge. In having the well-being of the citizens as his sole aim, the ideal politician functions as an 'expert', an analogy with another professional expert, the doctor, who judges what will deliver health – that is, order and proportion to the body.

Notable in this section is what Socrates asserts about music and tragic drama (501e–502d). For him, poetry, stripped of music, rhythm and metre, is a kind of oratory which, like oratory, panders to the desires of the mass of people ('tragic poets play the part of orators in their own world of the theatre', 502d2–3).

SOCRATES: Then let us go back once more to what I was saying to Polus and Gorgias. I maintained, if you remember, that
b there are some occupations which confine themselves to the production of pleasure without making any distinction

between better and worse, and others which are based on a knowledge of good and bad. I classed cookery as a knack rather than an art among the occupations which are concerned merely with pleasure, and the art of medicine among those which are concerned with good.

And by the god of friendship,[89] Callicles, I beg you not to suppose that you should joke with me, nor answer at random contrary to your real opinion, nor treat me as if I were joking, for you see that the subject we are discussing is one about which even a man of small intelligence should be seriously concerned; it is nothing less than how a person should live. Is he to adopt the life to which you invite me, doing what you call manly activities, speaking in the Assembly and practising oratory and engaging in politics on the principles at present in fashion among you politicians, or should he lead this life – that of a philosopher; and how does the latter life differ from the former? c

Perhaps the best course is to try to distinguish them, as I did a while ago, and when we have agreed, if we can, that these two lives really are distinct, to examine how they differ from one another and which is the one to be lived. But possibly you haven't yet grasped my meaning? d

CALLICLES: Indeed I haven't.

SOCRATES: Well, I will put it more clearly. Since you and I have agreed that there is such a thing as good and such a thing as pleasure, and that pleasure is different from good, and that there is a particular method to be practised in the acquisition of each, in the pursuit of pleasure and in the pursuit of good – But tell me first of all whether you agree with me on this point. Do you? e

CALLICLES: Yes.

SOCRATES: Well then, let me have your assent also to what I was saying to Gorgias and Polus, if I seemed to you then to be speaking the truth. I was saying that in my opinion cookery, unlike medicine, is a knack, not an art, and I added that, whereas medicine studies the nature of the patient before it treats him and knows the reasons which dictate its actions and can give a rational account of both, cookery on the other 501 hand approaches in a thoroughly unmethodical way even that pleasure which is the sole object of its care; it makes no study of the nature of pleasure or of the causes which produce it, but with practically no attempt at rational calculation simply preserves, as a matter of routine and experience, the b memory of what usually occurs, and produces its pleasures in this way.

Make up your mind then first of all whether this seems to you a satisfactory account of the matter, and whether the activities concerned with the soul may not be classified in a similar way, some of them proceeding from a scientific basis and exercising forethought for the welfare of the soul, while others neglect this and devote themselves entirely, like cookery in the other case, to the question of how to produce pleasure for the soul, without drawing any distinction between better and worse pleasures or caring about anything at all except the giving of gratification by any means, whether c for better or worse. I think, Callicles, that there are such activities, and I call everything of this sort pandering, whether it is concerned with the body or the soul or with anything else to which its aim is to give pleasure without any regard for what is better or worse. Do you subscribe to my opinion about this?

CALLICLES: I don't, Socrates; but I'm going along with you, in order to bring the discussion to a close and to oblige Gorgias here.

d SOCRATES: And is this pandering confined to a single soul, or can it be exercised on two or more?

CALLICLES: Clearly on two or more.

SOCRATES: Then it is quite possible to pander to the souls of a crowd, without regard to what is best for them?

CALLICLES: Yes, I suppose so.

SOCRATES: Can you tell me what are the activities which do this? Or, if you prefer, I will ask the questions and you say yes or no as I enumerate them. Let's take flute-playing first. e Do you regard this as an activity which aims only at giving us pleasure, with no thought for anything else?

CALLICLES: Yes, I do.

SOCRATES: And would you say the same of all such activities, playing the lyre at public competitions, for example?

CALLICLES: Yes.

SOCRATES: What about the training of choruses and dithyrambic poetry?[90] Would you put them in the same class? Do you suppose that Cinesias[91] the son of Meles worries whether his poetry is likely to improve his hearers, or only whether it will gratify the mass of the audience? 502

CALLICLES: Obviously the latter, Socrates, in the case of Cinesias anyway.

SOCRATES: And what about his father Meles?[92] Do you think he was aiming in his songs at what is best? Or even, for that matter, at giving maximum pleasure? His voice was agony to his audience. But, leaving that aside, don't you agree that singing to the lyre and dithyrambic poetry in general were invented to give pleasure?

CALLICLES: Yes.

SOCRATES: What of that solemn and marvellous creation, tragic drama? Is it the object of her earnest endeavour, in your opinion, simply to gratify the spectators, or does she strive to avoid anything that would harm them, however pleasant and attractive, and make it her business in dialogue and song to impart wholesome but unpalatable truths, whether the audience like it or not? For which of these purposes do you suppose that tragic poetry is adapted? b

CALLICLES: Obviously, Socrates, she aims more at giving pleasure and gratifying the audience. c

SOCRATES: Just what we declared a moment ago to be pandering, Callicles?

CALLICLES: Certainly.

SOCRATES: Now, if one were to strip all poetry of music, rhythm and metre, what is left would be mere words, would it not?

CALLICLES: Of course.

SOCRATES: And these words are addressed to a large mass of people?

CALLICLES: Yes.

SOCRATES: Then poetry is a sort of public speaking?

d CALLICLES: So it seems.

SOCRATES: In that case it would be oratory. Don't you think that the tragic poets play the part of orators in their own world of the theatre?

CALLICLES: Yes, I do.

SOCRATES: So now we have discovered a sort of oratory addressed to a mixed popular audience of children, women and men, slaves as well as free men; and oratory, moreover, of a kind which we don't much admire, seeing that by our account of the matter it is a species of pandering.

CALLICLES: I agree.

e SOCRATES: Good. Now, what are we to think of the oratory addressed to the Athenian people and to the assemblies of free men in other cities? Do the orators in your opinion speak always with an eye to what is best, and make it the constant aim of their speeches to improve their fellow-citizens as much as possible, or do they too set out merely to gratify the citizens, sacrificing the public interest to their own personal success, and treating the assemblies like children, whom their only 503 object is to please, without caring at all whether their speeches make them better or worse?

CALLICLES: There is no simple answer to this question as there was to the other, for some speakers are moved in their speeches by a regard for the public interest, and some are as you describe.

SOCRATES: I am content with that answer. Even if there are two kinds of political oratory, one of them, I suppose, would be pandering and shameful mass oratory; only the other is fine, which aims at making the souls of the citizens as good as possible and is always striving to say what is best, whether it is pleasing or not to the ears of the audience. But you have b never experienced the second type; or if you can point to any orator who conforms to it, why have you not let me into the secret? Who is he?

CALLICLES: By Zeus, I can't point to anyone of this kind among living speakers.

SOCRATES: Well then, is there anyone that you can name among the politicians of the past, from whose first public appearance one can date a change for the better in the character of the Athenians? For I don't know of any.

CALLICLES: What? Have you not heard that Themistocles was a good man, and Cimon and Militiades and Pericles?[93] The last died not so long ago, and you have heard him speak yourself. c

SOCRATES: Yes, Callicles, if what you were saying earlier is true, that being good consists in satisfying all the desires of oneself and others; but if it is not that, but, as we found ourselves driven to admit in our subsequent discussion, it consists in fulfilling those desires whose satisfaction makes someone better and denying those which make him worse, and if this is a matter of expert knowledge, can you point to any of these men who come up to this standard? d

CALLICLES: I don't know how to answer you.

SOCRATES: You will find an answer, if you look carefully.[94] So let us consider quite calmly whether any of the men you have named was of this type. Come now, the good man, who always aims at the best in what he says, will have some definite object in view will he not? He will no more proceed at random than other professional workers, each of whom chooses and employs means and materials with an eye to his particular task, in order that what he is fashioning may have a definite form. Take, for example, painters, builders, shipwrights, any other profession you like, and see how each of them arranges the different elements of his work in a certain order, and disciplines one part to fit and harmonize with another until the thing emerges a consistent and organized whole. Among other professional workers are those who deal with the body, trainers and doctors, whom we have already mentioned; they presumably give order and proportion to the body. Are we agreed that this is so or not? e 504

CALLICLES: We are agreed.

SOCRATES: Then whether a house is sound or in a bad condition will depend on whether it is built in accordance with order and proportion or not?

CALLICLES: Yes.

SOCRATES: And the same is true of a ship?

b CALLICLES: Yes.

SOCRATES: And also of our bodies?

CALLICLES: Certainly.

SOCRATES: What about the soul? Will the soundness of a soul consist in disorder or rather in a certain order and proportion?

CALLICLES: In the latter inevitably, if we are to be consistent.

SOCRATES: Now what do we call the quality which order and proportion give to the body?

CALLICLES: I suppose you mean health and strength?

c SOCRATES: Exactly so. And what is the quality which order and proportion create in the soul? Try to find a name for this, like the other.

CALLICLES: Why don't you answer your own question, Socrates?

SOCRATES: Well, I will, if you prefer it. But you must tell me whether you think I am right, and, if you don't, challenge me and not let the matter pass. In my opinion, 'healthy' is the name given to the means which produce order in the body, and their result is health and every other physical excellence. Is this so or not?

CALLICLES: It is so.

d SOCRATES: And the means which produce order and proportion in the soul are called 'regulation' and 'law'; these are what make men law-abiding and orderly, and so we have justice and moderation. Agreed?

CALLICLES: Very well.

SOCRATES: Then our orator, the good man of expert knowledge, will have these ends in view in any speech or action by which he seeks to influence the souls of men, in any gift which he may confer, and in any privation which he may inflict; he will always have his mind on how to bring justice and e moderation and every other virtue to birth in the souls of his fellow-citizens, and on removing their opposites, injustice and excess and vice. Do you agree or not?

CALLICLES: I agree.

SOCRATES: What point is there, Callicles, in giving plenty of the most delicious food and drink or whatever to an ailing and miserable body, when these will often do no more good than abstinence, or even, if the matter be rightly considered, even less good? Isn't that true?

CALLICLES: Assume it to be so. 505

SOCRATES: Yes, for I don't think it does someone any good to live with his body in misery; the inevitable outcome is a miserable life. Don't you agree?

CALLICLES: Yes.

SOCRATES: As far as satisfying one's appetites is concerned, eating as much as desired when one is hungry or drinking when one is thirsty, for example, this is generally allowed by doctors to a person in health, but an invalid is practically never permitted to have his fill of what he desires. Would even you concede this?

CALLICLES: Yes, I would.

SOCRATES: And is it not the same, my friend, with the soul? b As long as it is in a bad state, being ignorant, immoderate, immoral and irreligious, it must be restrained from satisfying its appetites and prevented from doing anything but what will improve it. Do you agree?

CALLICLES: Yes, I agree.

SOCRATES: Such a course is surely in the soul's own interest, is it not?

CALLICLES: Certainly.

SOCRATES: Isn't keeping it from what it desires the same thing as correcting it?

CALLICLES: Yes.

SOCRATES: Then correction is better for the soul than absence of restraint, which you preferred just now.

There are two aspects of this section of the dialogue needing further comment:

1. The 'craft-analogy'. *The analogy between 'arts' such as medicine (also translatable as 'crafts' (*technai *– see Glossary of Greek Terms)) and political activity is crucial for Plato's argument here and for the remainder of the dialogue; just as the doctor concerns himself with the health of the body of the patient and unquestionably has the expertise to do so, so the person practising the genuine art of politics has, by virtue of* *expertise, the power and authority to prescribe what is good for the souls of citizens. Since everybody really wants what is good for themselves – see B[2] above – just as anybody would want to be healthy rather than sick, what the genuine politician does, by virtue of his superior knowledge, is to show his 'patients' what is good for their souls. Furthermore, since an essential characteristic of genuine arts is to aim at 'order' (*kosmos*), so the political art has as its aim the 'order' of the soul, i.e. justice and moderation. However, all this follows if, and* only *if, one accepts the validity of the medicine/politics analogy; reliance on this analogy enables Socrates to avoid searching questions we might want to pose concerning political authority: can political questions (as Plato would say, matters of justice and injustice) be reduced to matters of expertise like, for example, medicine? And even if there are political experts, should power be given to them rather than, as in contemporary Athens, to the citizens as a whole? Callicles doesn't raise these objections, and it would not be in character for him to do so, because he no more supports the democratic ideal than Socrates, though, of course, for very different reasons (see* C[3] *above).*

2. Music and drama. *Unexpectedly introduced before the general discussion of politics, this section (501e–502d) appears to function as a digression from the main topic, but is in reality closely related to Socrates' critique of public oratory. As part of the cycle of Athenian religious festivals, artistic presentations and especially drama (502b1 ff.) took place before large audiences in the theatre, and were seen as public events, alongside meetings of the Assembly, involving a 'mass gathering' (*ochlos*). Despite the ironically expressed respect for tragedy (502b1), Plato has a consistently low regard for poetry as sharing the same shortcomings as oratory – a spurious art pandering to desires and not (or very rarely) aiming at the good. Plato elaborates his critique of poetry in* Republic, *Books 2, 3 and 10.*

C[7] 505c1–506c4

A short interlude which, like the others previously, is concerned with the course and conduct of the discussion.

CALLICLES: I don't know what you mean, Socrates; ask someone else. c

SOCRATES: We have here a man who cannot bear being improved and submitting in his own person to the correction that we are talking about.

CALLICLES: I don't feel the smallest interest in anything you say. My only motive in answering you was to oblige Gorgias.

SOCRATES: Well, what are we to do then? Leave the argument in the air?

CALLICLES: You must decide that for yourself.

SOCRATES: One ought not to leave even a story half told, they d say. It should be brought to a point and not left to go about pointless. So answer the rest of my questions, and let our discussion have a fitting end.

CALLICLES: What a bully you are, Socrates. If you take my advice you will let this discussion be, or argue with someone else.

SOCRATES: Who else would be willing? Don't let us leave the argument incomplete.

CALLICLES: Couldn't you finish the argument alone, either in a continuous speech or answering your questions yourself?

SOCRATES: 'One man doing the work of two', to quote Epich- e armus?[95] It looks as if it will have to be like that. But if we are to adopt this method, I think it must be on condition that we all regard ourselves as rivals in the attempt to distinguish truth from falsehood in what we say; we all benefit equally from the truth being made clear. So I will go through the argument myself as I see it; but if any of you think that I am 506 allowing myself to assume what is not true, he must interrupt and challenge me. I am not speaking from the certainty of assured knowledge; I am simply your fellow explorer in the search for truth, and if somebody contradicts me and there is something in what he says, I shall be the first to give way. This is all supposing that you decide that the argument should be continued to its end; otherwise let us give it up and go our separate ways.

GORGIAS: I don't think that we ought to leave, Socrates, until b you have finished the argument, and I am sure that the others agree with me.[96] Personally, I very much want to hear what more you yourself have to say.

SOCRATES: For my part, Gorgias, I should have liked to continue the discussion with Callicles, until I had paid him back a speech of Amphion for his Zethus.[97] However, since you won't collaborate any further, Callicles, at least listen and interrupt me if you don't agree with what I say. If you prove c your point, I shall not be annoyed with you as you were with me; on the contrary, I shall inscribe your name at the head of my list of benefactors.

CALLICLES: Go on, my friend, and finish on your own.

*Callicles' attitude to the debate reveals that the Socratic method of questioning has an emotional as well as an intellectual aspect: both questioner and the person questioned must be prepared to acknowledge demonstrable weaknesses and inconsistencies in their positions and be prepared to answer sincerely. Gorgias and Polus (in A and B) ostensibly have done this, but Callicles gradually shows himself deficient in both aspects; he wishes to leave the gathering (to avoid social or intellectual humiliation?) but stays, as he claims, under duress to oblige Gorgias and the assembled company. However, his unwillingness to take any further active part compels Socrates to answer himself (see 506c5 ff. below) and indulge in the long speeches (*makrologia*) for which he criticized Polus (B[1] above). Plato is perhaps also using Callicles' semi-withdrawal to signal a new phase of the dialogue, which allows Socrates to make a continuous exposition of his own point of view without the need for persuasion or coping with hostile interruption.*

C[8] 506c5–509a7

*Up to 507b5 Socrates acts as questioner and answerer, but then gives up the pretence of dialogue and embarks on a long speech in which he describes the good man as someone who possesses the virtue of self-discipline (*sophrosune *= 'moderation', 'self-control'), from which comes possession of the other traditional virtues: of justice (*dike *= correct behaviour towards other humans), reverence (*hosiotes *= correct behaviour towards the gods) and bravery (*andreia*). This is Socratic 'excellence' (*arete*). The licentious man (Callicles), lacking self-control, will consequently lack all these virtues, and so not possess* arete. *Socrates then introduces a new idea: that this moral order, which is found in the good person (he is 'well ordered' =* kosmios*), is a principle of order (*kosmos*) which unites all things in the universe; there is therefore no antithesis, as Callicles maintained (see C[1] above), between human and natural law (*nomos *and* physis*). From this Socrates concludes that Callicles was wrong when he claimed earlier (486a7 ff.) that Socrates' philosophy ('it is better to suffer than to do wrong') would leave him unable to defend himself against his enemies, which conventional Athenian* arete *would regard as the ultimate disgrace (*aischune*). More harm and so disgrace, Socrates maintains, is suffered by the wrongdoer. These conclusions are, Socrates asserts, universally true and 'bound fast by a chain of argument as strong as iron or adamant' (509a1–2).*

SOCRATES: Listen then, while I recapitulate the argument from the start. Is pleasure identical with good? Callicles and I agreed that it is not. – Is pleasure to be followed as a means to good or good as a means to pleasure? Pleasure as a means to good. – Is pleasure something whose presence makes us pleased, and good something whose presence makes us good? Certainly. – But we, and everything else that can be called good, are good by reason of the presence of some excellent quality, are we not? That seems an inevitable conclusion, Callicles. – Now the excellence of anything, whether d it be an implement or a physical body or a soul or any living being, is not manifested at random in its highest form, but springs from a certain order and rightness and art appropriate in each case. Is that true? In my opinion, yes. – Then the excellence of a thing depends on its having a certain organization and order which is the result of arrangement?

e

That is what I should say. – Consequently, the presence of the order proper to it is what makes each thing good? So I believe. – It follows that the soul which possesses the appropriate kind of order is better than the disorderly? Necessarily. – And a soul which possesses order is orderly? Of course. – And if orderly, disciplined by good sense? Unquestionably. – So the disciplined soul is good after all. I can't see any other conclusion, my dear Callicles, can you? Tell me if you can.

507

CALLICLES: Go on, my good fellow.

SOCRATES: I maintain that if a disciplined soul is good, a soul affected in the opposite way, which, as we have seen, is a soul marked by folly and licence, is bad. Certainly. – The man who is disciplined will behave with propriety towards gods and men; if he behaved improperly he would not deserve the name of disciplined. That is undeniable. – Again, proper behaviour toward men is justice and proper behaviour toward God reverence; and a man who acts justly and reverently must be just and reverent. Certainly. – And he must be brave as well; a disciplined man does not choose inappropriate objects either to pursue or to avoid; on the contrary, he will pursue or avoid the actions and people and pleasures and pains that deserve the appropriate course, and he will stand his ground firmly where duty requires it. It inevitably follows, Callicles, that the disciplined man whom we have described, being just and brave and reverent, is perfectly good; and a good man does well in all his actions, and because he does well[98] is happy and blessed, whereas the wicked man who does wrong is wretched. Such a person will be the opposite of the disciplined man, in fact the licentious man, who was the object of your encomium.

b

c

That then is the position that I adopt and maintain to be true. If it is true, then it appears that each of us who wants to be happy must pursue and practise self-discipline, and run as fast as his legs will carry him from licentiousness. He must d make it his main endeavour not to need correction, but if either he or anyone whom he relates to, be they individuals or a city, should stand in need of it, correction must be inflicted and the penalty paid if happiness is to be achieved.

This seems to me the goal that one should have in view throughout one's life; we can win happiness only by directing all our own efforts and those of the state to the realization of justice and self-discipline, not by allowing our desires to go e unchecked, and, in an attempt to satisfy them, evil without end, leading the life of an outlaw.

A person like this will win the love neither of god nor of his fellow-men; he is incapable of social life, and without social life there can be no friendship. Wise men say, Callicles, that heaven and earth, gods and men, are held together by 508 the bonds of community and friendship and order and discipline and righteousness, and that is why the universe, my friend, is called an ordered whole or cosmos and not a state of disorder and licence. You, I think, for all your cleverness, have not paid attention to these matters; you have not observed how great a part geometric equality plays among gods and men, and because you neglect the study of geometry you preach the doctrine of unfair shares.[99]

However that may be, the choice before you now is either to prove me wrong in my conviction that the happy owe their happiness to the possession of righteousness and discipline and the miserable owe their misery to the possession of vice, b or else, if what I say is true, to examine what follows from it. What follows, Callicles, are all those principles which you questioned my seriousness in stating when I said that in the event of any wrongdoing a man should be ready to accuse himself or his son or his friend, and that this was the end for which oratory should be employed.[100] It turns out after all that what you thought Polus admitted out of shame is true, and that doing wrong is not only more shameful than suffering wrong but also, in the same degree, more harmful to the doer; c and the man who is to be an orator in the proper sense must be just and understand right and wrong, which is what Polus in his turn accused Gorgias of being ashamed not to admit.[101]

In the light of all this, let us consider whether you are right or not when you reproach me with being unable to defend myself or any of my friends and relations or to save them from mortal danger, and assert that like an outlaw I am at d the mercy of anyone who chooses, if I may adopt your forcible expression, to slap me in the face, or deprive me of my property, or banish me from my city, or even, in the last resort, put me to death. To be in such a position is the lowest depth of disgrace, according to you; what my opinion is I have already stated several times, but it will bear repetition yet once more.

I maintain, Callicles, that it is not being slapped in the face e undeservedly, nor yet being wounded in my body or my purse that is the ultimate disgrace, but that it is more harmful as well as more disgraceful to strike and wound me and mine wrongfully; and that to rob me or enslave me or break into my house, or, generally speaking, to inflict any wrong upon me and mine brings more harm and disgrace upon the wrong-doer than upon those who suffer the wrong.

These conclusions, the soundness of which has already been demonstrated in our previous discussion, are, to speak somewhat boldly, held firm and bound fast by a chain of 509 argument as strong as iron or adamant, as far at any rate as I can judge at present; and unless you or someone more enterprising than you can undo this chain, no one who speaks differently from what I am saying can be right. For my part I follow my invariable principle; I do not claim to know that this is so, but I have never met anybody, present company included, who has produced a different opinion without making himself ridiculous.

There are two points of particular interest here:

1. Socrates takes the form *of the conventional Athenian value-system, but turns the* content *upside down:* arete *and the traditional virtues are invoked, but to support a set of values which contradict much of Athenian popular morality (as well as that of Callicles) – to do good to friends and evil to enemies (see B[3] above). It is also notable that Socrates here implies that the virtues are inseparable; if you have one (in this case* sophrosune *– 'self-discipline') you have them all. What is behind this, but not fully articulated in* Gorgias, *is the important Platonic idea of the unity of the virtues – they all amount to knowledge of good and evil (an idea hinted at in the discussion with Gorgias of 'arts' at A[6] above, and see the editorial comment there on Socrates' assumptions about the close association of virtue and knowledge).*

2. *Socrates' comments on the soundness of his line of argument emphasize how important he regards the 'chain' of agreement/disagreement to a succession of linked propositions. At the same time he concedes that it is only what they have established so far, and conclusions can be overturned by somebody who uses the Socratic method to prove otherwise. How does this emphasis on the provisional nature of the method square with the emphasis on arriving at the truth?*

C[9] 509a7–513c3

*That avoidance of suffering or doing wrong requires some kind of power or skill (*techne*) is a conclusion that Callicles can enthusiastically support ('See how ready I am to applaud you when you talk sense', 510a11–b1). But his half-agreements with Socrates have apparently not led him to realize that, for the latter, 'power' does not mean the capability and opportunity of imitating a tyrant, but acquiring a different sort of power, art or skill, similar to other more modest skills, such as those of navigation or engineering which, despite their lack of pretension and social prestige, achieve as much as conventional political skills. Callicles would be well advised to consider what skill will improve the quality of his life rather than give him the power to acquire wealth to prolong his existence at all costs.*

SOCRATES: I assume once more, therefore, that this is so, and if I am right and wrongdoing is the worst harm that can befall b a wrongdoer (though not to be punished for wrongdoing is even worse, if anything can be worse than the worst), what kind of protection will it really be ridiculous for a man not to be able to provide for himself? Surely protection against what does us the greatest harm. There can be no doubt whatever that it is the inability to provide this protection for oneself and one's friends and relations which brings the greatest c shame; second to this comes helplessness in the face of evil of the second degree of importance, and then of the third degree, and so on. The greater each evil is, the finer it is to have the power to mount a defence against it, and the more shameful it is to lack that power. Don't you agree, Callicles?

CALLICLES: Yes.

SOCRATES: Then of these two evils, doing wrong and suffering wrong, the former, we say, is the greater and the latter the less. Now, what equipment does a man need to ensure himself protection against both these evils, doing wrong and suffering d wrong alike? Is it power or will that is required? What I mean is this; will a man avoid suffering wrong simply by wanting not to suffer it, or must he obtain power in order to avert it?

CALLICLES: He must obtain power, obviously.

SOCRATES: But what about doing wrong? Is it sufficient assurance against wrongdoing not to wish to do wrong, or must a man, in this case too, equip himself with some sort of power e or skill, at the risk of being involved in wrongdoing if he fails to learn and practise it? Why haven't you answered me, Callicles, whether in your opinion Polus and I were right or not when we found ourselves forced to agree in our previous discussion that no one does wrong willingly and that all wrongdoing is involuntary.

510 CALLICLES: Take the point for granted, Socrates, if it will hasten the end of the discussion.

SOCRATES: Then it seems that if we are to avoid doing wrong we must acquire some sort of power or skill?

CALLICLES: Yes.

SOCRATES: What then is the skill which will protect us from suffering wrong or reduce that suffering to a minimum? Do you agree with me that it consists in holding office or even being a tyrant oneself, or else in being a friend of the existing government?

CALLICLES: Absolutely right, Socrates. See how ready I am to applaud you when you talk sense. b

SOCRATES: Consider then if this too is well said. I think that the closest friendship is that which exists between men whom the wise old proverb calls 'birds of a feather'?[102] Do you agree?

CALLICLES: Yes.

SOCRATES: So where power is in the hands of a savage and uneducated tyrant, anyone who is greatly his superior will doubtless be an object of fear to the ruler, and never able to be on terms of genuine friendship with him. c

CALLICLES: That is true.

SOCRATES: And the same applies to anyone greatly his inferior. In that case the tyrant will despise him and never regard him with the esteem due to a friend.

CALLICLES: That is equally true.

SOCRATES: Then the only man left worth consideration for the tyrant to make a friend of is the man of similar character to himself, who agrees with his likes and dislikes and is willing to obey him and submit to his authority. He is the man who will have great power in this city; it is he that no one will injure with impunity, is it not? d

CALLICLES: Yes.

SOCRATES: So if a young man in that city were to ask himself: 'How can I get great power and have no one wrong me?', the way would seem to lie in accustoming himself from an early age to share the likes and dislikes of his master, and in modelling himself upon him as closely as possible. Agreed?

CALLICLES: Yes.

SOCRATES: Such a man will have achieved the goal of not being wronged and of possession of great power in the city, as you e and your friends would argue.

CALLICLES: Certainly.

SOCRATES: But will he also have secured himself against the danger of inflicting wrong? Far from it, if the master on whom he is to model himself and whose favour he enjoys is *himself* a wrongdoer. His own efforts will, I think, be directed in quite the opposite direction – to do as much wrong as possible and not be punished for the wrongdoing. Isn't that so?

CALLICLES: Apparently.

511 SOCRATES: In that case there will befall him the greatest of all evils: a soul depraved and corrupted by the imitation of his master and the power thus acquired.

CALLICLES: Somehow or other, Socrates, you always contrive to turn things upside down. Don't you know that the imitator we are speaking of will kill your non-imitator, if he chooses, and take away his property?

b SOCRATES: I should have to be deaf not to know it, my good Callicles, seeing how often I have heard it, from you and from Polus several times before you, and from practically everyone else in Athens. But let me tell you, on the other hand, that your man may kill, if he chooses, but he will be a villain killing a good and honourable man.

CALLICLES: Isn't that exactly what is so infuriating?

SOCRATES: Not to a man of sense, as can easily be proved. Do you think that a man ought to make it his chief ambition to prolong his life to the utmost limit, and spend it in the practice of the arts which constantly preserve us from danger – ora-c tory, for example, which you advise me to cultivate as a protection in the law courts?

CALLICLES: And very sound advice it is too, by Zeus!

SOCRATES: Well, my good fellow, do you also regard ability to swim as an impressive accomplishment?

CALLICLES: By Zeus, no.

SOCRATES: Yet even swimming saves men from death, whenever they get into a situation that requires that knowledge. But if swimming seems to you a triviality, take a more important d branch of knowledge, navigation, which, like oratory, saves not only people's lives from extreme danger but also the persons and property which belong to them. Navigation is a modest art that knows her place; she does not put on airs or make out that she has performed some brilliant feat, even though she achieves as much as forensic oratory; she brings people safe from Aegina for no more than two obols, I believe, and even if they come from Egypt or Pontus or ever so far away, the very most she charges for this great service, for conveying in safety, as I said, a man and his children and property and women, is two drachmae[103] when he disembarks at the Piraeus; and the man who possesses this skill and has accomplished all this lands and walks about on the shore beside his ship in a quite unassuming way. e

The reason is, I imagine, that he is sensible enough to see that it is quite uncertain which of his passengers he has done a service to by not allowing them to be drowned and which the reverse; he knows that he has landed them in no better condition, in body or soul, than when they embarked. So he reflects that, if he has done no good to a man suffering from serious and incurable physical ailments, who is simply to be pitied because he has not gone to the bottom, still less can life be held to be a boon to a man who has a mass of incurable diseases in his soul, which is so much the more precious part of him; it is doing no service to such a man to save him from the sea or the law court or any other danger, the truth being, as the skipper knows, that there is no advantage to the wicked man in continuing to live, seeing that he cannot live other than badly. 512 b

That is why the skipper, although he saves our lives, is not in the habit of magnifying his office; and the same may be said, my friend, of the engineer, whose ability to save is as great as that of a general or anyone else, let alone a skipper, for an engineer sometimes saves whole cities. You wouldn't think of putting him on the same level as the advocate, would you? Yet if he chose to boast about his profession, like you and your friends, Callicles, he could make out a strong case and overwhelm you with reasons why everybody ought to be an engineer and other pursuits are of no use at all. All the same, you despise him and his art and use the term 'engineer' as a term of contempt, and you would not hear of marrying your daughter to his son or taking his daughter yourself.[104] c

Yet, to go simply by the argument which you advance in praise of your own way of life, what right have you to despise d the engineer and the others I have just mentioned? You will say, I know, that you are a better man and better born. But if 'better' has a different meaning from the meaning I give it, and the height of goodness consists in keeping oneself and one's property safe, regardless of one's character, it is simply absurd for you to cast aspersions on engineering and medicine and the other professions which exist in order to ensure people's safety. But I beg you, my friend, to reflect whether nobility and goodness may be something different from keeping oneself and others alive, and to consider whether a true man, instead of clinging to life at all costs, ought not to e dismiss from his mind the question how long he may have to live. Let him leave that to the will of God in the belief that the women are right when they tell us that no man can escape his destiny,[105] and let him devote himself to the next problem, how he can best live the life which is allotted to him, and whether he will achieve this by adapting himself to the constitution of the state in which he happens to live. In that case it 513 will be your duty at the present time to model your character as closely as possible on the character of the Athenian people, if you are to gain their affection and acquire great power in the city. Ask yourself whether such a course is really to the advantage of either of us, and take care, my good friend, that we do not suffer the reputed fate of the witches of Thessaly who draw the moon down from the sky;[106] that we do not find, I mean, that we have purchased political power at the cost of all we hold most dear.

If you believe, Callicles, that anyone can pass on to you a skill which will make you powerful in the city, and yet remain, b whether for better or worse, unlike it in character, you are in my opinion quite mistaken. It is not a matter of imitation; there must be a genuine natural likeness if you are to make any real progress in the affections of the Athenian *demos*, or, by Zeus, of Pyrilampes'[107] Demos either. So whoever can fashion you to be most like them is the man who can help you to realize your political ambitions and make you an orator; each demos takes pleasure in hearing sentiments which are in c harmony with its own nature and detests the reverse. I speak subject to your correction, my dear friend, but is there in fact anything to be said against this conclusion, Callicles?

Socrates here breaks no new philosophical ground, but reworks the old arguments with Polus (B above) in order gradually to broaden the canvas; at the end of the section it becomes clear that he is no longer talking about faraway tyrants like Archelaus of Macedon but about the Athenian people and Callicles' devotion to their desires.

C[10] 513c4–517c4

As with his own life, so the effect of the budding politician on others needs to be examined. If, as Socrates claims, politics is a techne *and as such aims at the good of those on whom it is practised (C[6] above), the political practitioner will need to show that he has that* techne. *Just as the builder or doctor standing for a public appointment will need to point to successful projects or cured patients (i.e. produce his CV, as it were), so, before embarking on a public career, Callicles will need to demonstrate that he has made somebody better. Famous politicians of the immediate past do not meet the criterion; they did not make their citizens better, since those citizens turned against them. If those politicians had made them good, the citizens could not have turned against them. On the other hand, the politicians cannot be classified as successful panders either, since their ultimate unpopularity shows that they did not give the citizens what they wanted.*

CALLICLES: Somehow or other I can't help being impressed by what you say, Socrates; yet, like most other people, I am not completely convinced.

SOCRATES: That is because the love of Demos in your soul, Callicles, is putting up a resistance to my argument, but perhaps if we go over the same ground many times you will be convinced. Remember now that we said that body and soul can each of them be treated in two different ways; one d aims at pleasure, the other at what is best, not giving in but putting up a fight. Isn't that the distinction which we drew at an earlier stage?[108]

CALLICLES: Certainly.

SOCRATES: And the former method, whose aim is pleasure, is dishonourable and simply a form of pandering, is it not?

e CALLICLES: Call it so if you like.

SOCRATES: Whereas the latter aims at producing the greatest degree of good in body and soul, whichever is the object of our treatment.

CALLICLES: Certainly.

SOCRATES: Ought we not then to set about our treatment of the city and its citizens on this principle, with the idea of making the citizens themselves as good as possible? For without such a principle, as we discovered earlier, one can do no good; no other service to the state is of the slightest avail if 514 those who are to acquire riches or authority over people, or any other kind of power, are not men of goodwill. Can we agree that this is so?

CALLICLES: Yes, if you prefer.

SOCRATES: Suppose, now, Callicles, that in some undertaking for the city we were advising one another on a building contract for the most important type of public works, walls or dockyards or temples. Would it or would it not be our duty first of all to examine ourselves and ask whether or not b we understood the art of building and from whom we had learnt it?

CALLICLES: It would be our duty of course.

SOCRATES: And a second question would be whether we had ever put up any private building either for a friend or for ourselves, and, if so, whether that building were beautiful or ugly. If it appeared on investigation that we had had good c and reputable masters and had put up many fine buildings, both in collaboration with them and on our own after we ceased to be their pupils, it would be sensible in those circumstances to venture upon public works. But if, on the other hand, we could give the name of no master and point to no buildings standing to our credit, or only to many buildings, but devoid of all merit, it would surely be senseless to set our hand to public works and to urge one another to do so. Is that right or not? d

CALLICLES: Quite right.

SOCRATES: It is the same with everything. Suppose, for example, that in the belief that we were competent doctors you and I were urging each other to stand for a public medical appointment. Presumably we should submit ourselves to mutual examination along these lines: 'Tell me, by the gods, what is Socrates' own state of physical health? Has anybody, whether slave or free, ever been cured of a disease by Socrates' treatment?' I should ask the same sort of questions about you, I think, and if we found that nobody, foreigner or native, man or woman, had ever got better through our treatment, then e by Zeus, Callicles, shouldn't we make ourselves really ridiculous if we were such fools as to attempt to obtain public office ourselves and to advise people like us to do the same, before we had first served a long apprenticeship of trial and error, followed by considerable successful experience of our profession in private practice? We should be like the man in the proverb who began his apprenticeship as a potter by trying his hand at a wine-jar.[109] Don't you think that such behaviour would be senseless?

CALLICLES: Yes, I do.

SOCRATES: Now, let us take our own position, my friend. You 515 have lately embarked on a public career and are urging me to do the same and reproaching me for my reluctance. Surely then this is the moment for mutual examination. Come now, has any citizen hitherto become a better man through the influence of Callicles? Is there anyone, foreign or native, slave or free, who owes to Callicles his conversion to virtue from a previous wicked career of wrongdoing and debauchery and folly? What will you say if you are asked this question, Callicles? What example will you give of a man who has been b improved by associating with you? Why hesitate to answer, if you can point to any achievement of yours in this line while you were still a private person, before you entered politics?

CALLICLES: You're always set upon victory, Socrates.

SOCRATES: Not at all; I'm not asking you just to win the argument, but because I genuinely want to know how you think our political life should be conducted. Surely your sole c concern in going into politics will be to make us who are citizens as good as possible. Have we not already agreed more than once that this is the duty of the statesman? Have we agreed? Answer, yes or no? Well, I will answer for you; we *have* agreed. Then if this is the service which a good man owes to his city, turn your mind once more to the people you mentioned a while ago, Pericles and Cimon and Miltiades d and Themistocles, and tell me whether you still think that they were good citizens.

CALLICLES: I do.

SOCRATES: In that case each of them must clearly have left the citizens better than he found them. Did he do so or not?

CALLICLES: Yes, he did.

SOCRATES: Then when Pericles first appeared on a public platform, the citizens were in a worse state than when he made his last speeches.

CALLICLES: Perhaps.

SOCRATES: It isn't a question of perhaps, my friend; it is a necessary consequence of what we have agreed, if he really was a good citizen.

e CALLICLES: What of it, then?

SOCRATES: Nothing; but just tell me this as well: are the Athenians supposed to have been improved by Pericles' influence or, on the contrary, to have been corrupted by him? The latter is what I hear; people say that Pericles made the Athenians lazy and cowardly and garrulous and greedy by his introduction of the system of payment for services to the city.

CALLICLES: The people who tell you that are pro-Spartans with cauliflower ears,[110] Socrates.

SOCRATES: There is one thing, however, that I know positively from my own experience, not just from hearsay, and so do you. At the beginning of his career Pericles' reputation was high, and no sentence for disgraceful conduct was ever passed on him by the Athenians, who were worse at that time than they subsequently became; but when he had converted them to virtuous ways, at the end of his life, they convicted him of embezzlement and came near to condemning him to death, obviously because they believed him to be evil.[111] 516

CALLICLES: What of that? Does that make Pericles a bad man?

SOCRATES: Well, we should have a poor opinion of a man in charge of asses or horses or cattle, who took over the animals free from any tendency to kick or butt or bite him, but handed them back in a ferocious state, doing all these things. Don't you think that any man is a bad keeper of any animal, whatever it may be, who leaves it fiercer than he found it? b Yes or no?

CALLICLES: Yes, to please you.

SOCRATES: Please me again then with an answer to this question too: is a human being one of the animals or not?

CALLICLES: Of course he is.

SOCRATES: And Pericles was in charge of human beings?

CALLICLES: Yes.

SOCRATES: Well then, if Pericles looked after them as a good statesman should, ought not his charges to have become more virtuous and less vicious under his influence? That is what we c agreed just now.

CALLICLES: Certainly.

SOCRATES: And according to Homer the virtuous are gentle.[112] What do you say? Isn't this so?

CALLICLES: Yes.

SOCRATES: And yet Pericles made his charges fiercer than when he took them on, and, what is more, fiercer towards himself, which is the last thing he would have wished.

CALLICLES: Do you want me to agree?

SOCRATES: If what I am saying seems true to you.

CALLICLES: Very well, let it be so.

SOCRATES: Now, if they were fiercer, they were more vicious and less good.

CALLICLES: Granted. d

SOCRATES: Then by this reason Pericles was not a good statesman.

CALLICLES: That is what *you* say.

SOCRATES: So do you, by Zeus, on your own admission. But

tell me now about Cimon. Did not the people whom he was caring for ostracize him in order that they might not hear his voice for ten years?[113] And they did the same to Themistocles, and punished him with exile[114] besides. As for Miltiades of Marathon, they condemned him to be thrown into the pit e appointed for criminals, and, but for the President of the Council, that is what would have happened to him.[115] Yet if these people were good men, as you assert, this sort of thing would never have happened to them. You never find a good charioteer who begins by keeping his balance, and later, when he has trained his horses and increased his own expertise, then comes to grief. That simply does not happen, either in driving or in any other activity. Do you think it does?

CALLICLES: No, I don't.

SOCRATES: It seems then that what we said before is true, that 517 we know of no one who has been a good statesman in this city. You admitted that there is none now living, but declared that there had been such in the past and selected these four men. But now it appears that they were no better than the men of our time, and if they were orators the oratory that they employed was neither the genuine kind – in that case they would not have fallen from power – nor the kind which we have called pandering.

CALLICLES: But yet, Socrates, none of the men today comes b anywhere near equalling the achievements of any of the four men in question.

SOCRATES: My dear friend, I find no more fault with them than you do as servants of the city; indeed they seem to me to have been better servants than the present people, and more able to provide the city with what it desired. But when it is a matter of diverting people's desires into a new channel instead of allowing them free play, or of driving one's fellows by persuasion or constraint to adopt measures designed for their improvement, which is the sole duty of a good citizen, there is practically nothing to choose between your men and their successors, though I grant you that the men of old were c cleverer than our contemporaries in providing ships and walls and dockyards and the like.[116]

Socrates' theory of political rule does not fit the historical facts of the careers of Pericles, Cimon, Miltiades or Themistocles (note the uneasy 'halfway house' in which he situates them, at 517a5–6, between genuine statesmanship and pandering). Pericles' actions in particular were at least in part dictated by the need to persuade the Athenians to agree to a course of action which was initially unpleasant (abandonment of the territory of Attica at the beginning of the Peloponnesian War (431 BC) and confinement of the population within the walls of the city) in order to gain ascendancy over Sparta (see Thucydides, History of the Peloponnesian War, *Book 2). Likewise, before the Persian Wars earlier in the fifth century (483 BC), the statesman Themistocles' proposal to use a lucky strike of silver from the Laureion mines (on the southern tip of Attica) to build up a navy to face the Persians (Herodotus 7.144) had to compete against the much more immediately attractive proposal to distribute the money among the people.*

The mismatch between Socrates' schematic theory of rule in terms of moral values and the complications of historical reality arises from his failure, or, more likely, unwillingness to recognize that political leadership, and opposition to it, can involve practical and strategic decisions as well as moral imperatives, and that lack of success may not necessarily (as Socrates assumes in Pericles' case at 516a1–3) be attributable to moral failure. Underlying Socrates' comments on Pericles et al., however, is Plato's fundamental opposition to democracy. This is partly political prejudice – note the equation in 515e4–7 of Pericles' introduction of pay for political services with cowardice and laziness, and the implication that the provision of 'ships and walls and dockyards and the like' (517c2–3), was the mere gratification of desires (pandering to the populace) rather than foresighted military policy. Yet Plato's position is not entirely prejudice but follows from his belief that these political matters, like technical subjects, are the province of the expert, whose automatic aim for the betterment of his subjects gives him not only the right but the duty to impose his will on them. Democracy – everybody, not just the expert, having a say and a vote, and rulers taking note of what the ordinary (non-expert) person says and wants – is directly contrary to this.

C[11] 517c4–522e8

*Socrates now brings to bear on the politicians the schematic distinction between genuine and spurious arts which he drew right at the beginning of his discussion with Polus (B[1] above). Note, however, that the dichotomy here is not entirely consistent with the earlier one: in consideration of the body, cookery and baking, previously regarded as 'knacks' (see above 462c3 ff.), now appear to have the status of 'arts' (*technai*, 517e6–7), but as subordinate to the superior arts of the doctor and trainer which give them their proper direction. The problem with politicians is that, instead of caring for people's souls by employing the directive arts (their proper job, according to Plato), they act like unregulated practitioners of the subordinate arts and serve the citizens' unhealthy desires. Socrates then puts his own gloss on the 'good old days': far from favourably contrasting the past with the present, he sees the 'diet' served up by the revered politicians of the past as the real cause of the current 'illness'.*

Developing a point introduced in the previous section (C[10] above, in connection with the fifth-century politicians), Socrates enlarges on the question of the ill-treatment of teachers: they cannot complain because if the teacher is successful in teaching virtue, the pupil will not (cannot) inflict anything bad on them in return. Hence, unlike other arts, the teacher of virtue need not charge his pupils a fee because he need have no worry about unfair treatment at their hands. This issue (Socrates was distinguished from other teachers in giving his services free) leads on to the climax of the argument – Socrates' representation of himself as the only true statesman, in which his parody of the trial of a doctor 'brought before a jury of children with a cook as prosecutor' (521e3–4) foreshadows, in comic form, his own fate. The subject of death and its relation to the kind of life lived (522d7 ff.) leads into the final section of the dialogue.

SOCRATES: Discussion between you and me is an absurd affair; all the time we have been talking we have never ceased to revolve in an endless circle of mutual misunderstanding. All the same, I believe that on several occasions you have admitted and realized that dealing with the human body and the human soul is a twofold business. One way of proceeding is to behave as a servant; that is how the body is provided with food when it is hungry, drink when it is thirsty, clothes, blankets and shoes when it is cold, and has all its other desires satisfied as they arise; I am purposely using the same illustrations in order to make it easier for you to grasp. The supplier of these needs may be a shopkeeper or a merchant or the actual producer of one of the articles in question – a baker or cook or weaver or shoemaker or tanner; it is no wonder, if such people become possessed with the idea that they are responsible for the body's welfare and inspire the same belief in others, in everyone in fact who does not know that besides all these occupations there exist the arts of the trainer and the doctor, and that these constitute genuine care of the body; it is their province to control all these other arts and make use of their products, because they alone know what kinds of food and drink have a tendency to promote physical well-being or the reverse. This is a subject of which the other crafts are entirely ignorant, and that is why among the occupations that deal with the body they should be classed as servile and menial and unworthy of free men, whereas the arts of training and medicine have every right to be their mistresses. d e 518

When I tell you that the same situation exists with regard to the soul, you sometimes seem to understand and express agreement as if you know what I mean, but a moment later you come out with an assertion that excellent men are to be found among the citizens of this city, and whenever I ask you who they are, the names of the politicians you bring forward are such as to make me think that, if my question were about physical training and I asked you to give the names of good authorities past or present on care of the body, you would answer quite seriously that Thearion the baker and Mithaecus the author of the Sicilian cookery book and Sarambus[117] the b

shopkeeper are wonderful authorities on care of the body,
c because the first produces wonderful cakes, the second sauces and the third wine.

Probably you would be annoyed with me if I were to say to you: 'Fellow, you know nothing at all about physical training. The people you mention are servants and caterers to the desires, devoid of any sound or true knowledge of their nature; they are the sort of people who may well win people's praise by cramming and fattening their bodies, and afterwards cause them to lose even the flesh they had; and the victims of
d their ignorance instead of holding the suppliers of their feasts responsible for their ailments and loss of weight, will throw the blame on whoever happen to be their associates and advisers at a considerably later date, when their surfeit in defiance of the laws of health brings sickness in its train. These are the people they will blame, reproach and injure if they can, while they continue aloud in the praises of those others who are the real authors of their troubles.'

e You now, Callicles, are behaving in just the same way as these gluttons: you are extolling men who have regaled the Athenians by giving them their fill of what they desired, and people say that they have made Athens great; what they do not perceive is that through the efforts of these earlier
519 statesmen it is festering and rotten to the core. They have glutted the state with harbours and dockyards and walls and tribute and rubbish of that sort, taking no account of moderation and justice, and when the inevitable fit of weakness supervenes, the citizens will hold their current advisers responsible, and go on extolling Themistocles and Cimon and Pericles, the real authors of their woes. Possibly, when they begin to lose their old possessions as well as their current acquisitions, they will, if you are not careful, even attack you[118] and my friend Alcibiades, both of whom may perhaps
b share some responsibility for the crisis, though you were not its originators.

There is one piece of folly which I see being practised today besides hearing it reported from earlier times. Whenever the city attempts to bring any of its politicians to account as wrongdoers, I find that they take it very hard and raise a great outcry that they are being monstrously treated; their argument is that, after all the benefits they have conferred on the state, it is most unfair that they should come to ruin at its hands. Now, all that is a straight lie. No city leader could ever have ruin inflicted on him by the very state over which he presides unless he deserved it. The same seems to be true of c those who profess to be statesmen or sophists, for sophists, for all their wisdom, are guilty of this absurdity: professing to be teachers of virtue they often accuse their pupils of wronging them by cheating them of their fees and in other ways not making a proper return for the benefits they have received. What can be more illogical than to suppose that d men who have become good and upright by losing their tendency to wrongdoing, and by acquiring righteousness through the teaching of their master, should commit wrong by the exercise of a quality that they no longer possess? Don't you think that absurd, my friend? By your refusal to answer you have compelled me to hold forth like a true demagogue, Callicles.

CALLICLES: And you couldn't speak unless someone answered you?

SOCRATES: Apparently I can; on this occasion anyhow, since e you refuse to answer, I'm stretching out my speech to inordinate length. But tell me for friendship's sake, my good man, don't you think it absurd for someone who claims to have made somebody virtuous to find fault with his convert for being a scoundrel, when he has become virtuous under his instruction and still remains so?

CALLICLES: I certainly do.

SOCRATES: And don't you frequently hear those who profess to instruct people in virtue making this sort of complaint?

CALLICLES: Yes, I do; but why waste words? They are not 520 worth bothering about.

SOCRATES: Then what would you say of those who profess to guide the state and to make it as good as possible, but yet are quite ready to accuse it of supreme wickedness when occasion arises? Are they any better than the people I have mentioned?

The fact is, my dear fellow, as I was saying to Polus, there is practically nothing to choose between the sophist and the orator; it is merely ignorance that makes you regard the latter

b as beyond praise and despise the former.[119] In actual truth, the art of the sophist ranks as far above oratory as legislation above the administration of justice or physical culture above medicine. But it has always appeared to me that public orators and sophists are the only people who can't blame the subjects of their instruction for behaving badly towards them, unless they are prepared to accuse themselves of not having delivered the benefit they claimed to. Isn't that so?

c CALLICLES: Undoubtedly.

SOCRATES: And they are also the only people presumably who could reasonably be expected to give their services free if what they profess is true. In any other case of a service rendered, as when, for instance, a man improves his pace as a runner through a trainer, there is a possibility that the pupil might cheat the expert of his due if the latter gave his services free, without entering into a contract in advance and receiving payment as nearly as possible at the time he imparts the secret

d of speed. For I think, of course, that it is not slowness of foot but a tendency to wrongdoing that causes people to do wrong?

CALLICLES: Yes.

SOCRATES: So if someone removes that very quality, wrongdoing, he is in no danger of being wronged; he is the only person who could safely give his services free, provided that he really possessed the ability to make people good. Isn't that so?

CALLICLES: I agree.

SOCRATES: Presumably that is why there is no discredit in a man receiving payment for his advice on any other subject, building, for instance, or some similar art?

e CALLICLES: Presumably.

SOCRATES: But when one is dealing with the question how a person might have as good a character as possible and best manage either his own household or the city, it is reckoned discreditable, isn't it, to refuse to give advice except for payment?

CALLICLES: Yes.

SOCRATES: Obviously the reason is that this is the only service which makes the recipient eager to make a return in kind; so if the performer of the service gets back the same treatment as he gave, it is good evidence that his efforts have been successful, and vice versa. Is that not so?

CALLICLES: It is. 521

SOCRATES: Then distinguish for me which kind of care you would urge me to apply to the city. Am I to do battle with the Athenians with the intention of making them as good as possible, like a doctor, or to behave like a servant whose aim is to please? Tell me the truth, Callicles; you began by speaking your mind frankly, and I have a right to expect you to continue to say what you think; so now speak out loud and clear.

CALLICLES: What I say then is that you should be the city's servant.

SOCRATES: So in fact you are urging me, my most noble fellow, to be a pander. b

CALLICLES: Yes, if you prefer to be offensive.[120] Otherwise –

SOCRATES: Don't tell me once more that my life will be at the mercy of anyone who pleases. Save me the trouble of repeating that in this case 'an evil man will kill a good'; nor yet that I shall be stripped of my possessions, or I shall tell you again that the man who strips me will gain nothing from his booty. Having acquired it by wrong he will make a wrong use of it, and wrong involves shame, and shame wickedness. c

CALLICLES: You seem to me, Socrates, to be as confident that none of these things will happen to you as if you were living in another world and were not liable to be dragged into court, possibly by some vile scoundrel.

SOCRATES: I should truly be a fool, Callicles, if I didn't realize that in this city anything may happen to anybody. But of this at least I am sure, that, if I am brought to trial on a charge involving any of the penalties you mention, my prosecutor will be an evil man, for no honest man would prosecute an d innocent party. And it would not be at all surprising if I were executed. Would you like to know why I expect this?

CALLICLES: Very much.

SOCRATES: I believe that I am one of the few Athenians – perhaps indeed the only one – who studies the true political art, and that I alone of my contemporaries put it into practice. So because what I say on any occasion is not designed to please, and because I aim not at what is most agreeable but e at what is best, and will not employ those 'niceties'[121] which you advise, I shall have no defence to offer in a court of law. I can only repeat what I was saying to Polus; I shall be judged like a doctor brought before a jury of children with a cook as prosecutor. Imagine what sort of defence a man like that could make before such a court if he were accused in the following terms: 'Children, this man here has done many bad things to you and hurts even the youngest of you – he cuts and burns you, he squeezes and strangles you until you are 522 helpless, gives you horrible medicines and forces you to be hungry and thirsty. Now look at me – I put on parties for you, with lots of sweets and all kinds of goodies.' What do you think the doctor would be able to say, caught up in this dreadful situation? If he told the truth: 'I did all this, children, because I wanted to make you healthy', don't you think that a jury like that would make an uproar, and shout pretty loudly?[122]

CALLICLES: Perhaps.

SOCRATES: We must think so.[123] And then don't you think that b the accused would be at his wit's end for a reply?

CALLICLES: No doubt he would.

SOCRATES: Well, that is the situation in which I am sure that I should find myself if I came before a court of law. I shall not be able to point to any pleasures that I have provided for my judges, the only kind of service and good turn that they recognize; indeed I see nothing to envy either in those who give or those who receive such services. And if it is alleged against me either that I ruin younger people by reducing them to a state of helpless doubt or that I insult their elders by bitter criticism in public or in private, I will not be able to speak the truth: 'all that I say is right and I am simply acting in your c interests, gentlemen of the jury' – or anything else. So presumably I shall have no alternative but to submit to my fate, whatever it may be.

CALLICLES: Do you really think, Socrates, that all is well with a man in such a position who cannot defend himself before his city?

SOCRATES: I do think so, Callicles, provided that he has at his disposal the one form of self-defence whose strength you have yourself frequently acknowledged: the defence which consists in never having done wrong to gods or men either in word or deed. This, as we have agreed more than once, is the best of all kinds of self-defence. If it were proved against me that I was incapable of procuring for myself or helping others to procure this sort of defence, I should be ashamed, whether the tribunal which convicted me were large or small, or even if it were simply one to one. If this incapacity were to be the cause of my death I should feel great distress; but if I were to come to my end for lack of the pander's type of oratory, I am sure that you would see me facing my fate with serenity. The mere act of dying has no terror for anyone who is not completely without sense and manliness; it is wrongdoing that is to be feared; for to enter the next world with one's soul loaded with wrongdoing is the ultimate of all evils. I would like to tell you an account of how this is so, if you wish.

d

e

CALLICLES: Well, since you have finished with all your other points, you may as well round things off.

Particularly significant in this section is Plato's dual focus on historical events: Socrates in dramatic context (late fifth century) is looking back on Pericles (and Cimon) as leaders he would have experienced first-hand; the much younger Plato, at the time of composition (380s), has a longer perspective, including the crucial defeat of 404 BC and its political aftermath, which he tells us (see the Introduction, 'Socrates and Plato') had a profound effect on him. So, hindsight on the fate of Athens and Socrates' friend Alcibiades can be presented as foresight at 519a. More crucially, this dual focus contributes to the dramatic intensity with which Socrates refers forward to (and Plato looks back on) his trial and condemnation on a charge of impiety.

This, incidentally, reveals an aspect of the situation which seems to have escaped Plato: Socrates, despite presenting himself as perhaps the only Athenian who studied the true political art (521d6–8), failed, on the criteria he insisted on for Pericles et al., to teach the Athenians well enough and so make them good enough, to prevent their prosecuting and condemning him. *An ironic parallel to Pericles?*

C[12] 523a1–527e7

*The dialogue concludes with an account (*logos*) of the afterlife, in which Socrates departs radically from the argumentative mode sustained up to this point. The story, which Socrates maintains is true (it is not just a 'legendary tale' (*muthos*: 523a2), is assembled by Plato from a variety of details from traditional Greek myths of the afterlife found in Homer, Pindar (fifth-century* BC *Theban lyric poet), Aristophanes and Pythagorean and Orphic sources, but given an original thrust – the belief that individuals will receive rewards and punishments after death strictly commensurate with their actual conduct in life. Individuals will not be able to maintain any deception; they will come before the judging deities naked, with the signs of how they have spent their lives clearly visible not only on their bodies but on their souls. Punishment is meted out, with the aim of either improvement or (in the case of those who are deemed incurable) as an example to others. Rewards and punishments reverse apparent injustices in life: the evil tyrant will not ultimately be 'happy', 'prosperous' (*eudaimon*) and the virtuous sufferers will have their favourable reward. Callicles, if he does not mend his ways, will be as helpless before the divine tribunal as Socrates will be before his earthly judges. Socrates concludes by reasserting the main argument of the dialogue: 'this conclusion alone stands firm: that one should avoid doing wrong with more care than being wronged, and that the supreme object of a man's efforts, in public and in private life, must be the reality rather than the appearance of goodness' (527b3–7).*

SOCRATES: Give ear then, as they say, to a very fine story, which will, I suppose, seem just a legendary tale to you but is fact to me; what I am going to tell you I tell you as the truth.[124] 523

Homer relates that, when they succeeded their father, Zeus and Poseidon and Pluto divided his empire between them.[125] Now, there was in the time of Kronos a law concerning mankind which has remained in force among the gods from that time to this. The law ordains that, when his time comes to die, a man who has lived a righteous and holy life shall depart to the Isles of the Blessed and there live in complete happiness, free from evils, but that the man whose life has been wicked and godless shall be imprisoned in the place of retribution and judgement, which is called Tartarus. b

In the time of Kronos and in the early days of the reign of Zeus humans were tried while still alive by living judges on the very day on which they were fated to die. This led to wrong verdicts, so Pluto and the overseers of the Isles of the Blessed came to Zeus and complained that people were arriving at both destinations contrary to what they deserved. Then Zeus said: 'I will put an end to this. At present verdicts are wrongly given. The cause of this is that men are being tried in their clothes, for they are still alive when this happens.[126] Many whose souls are wicked are dressed in the trappings of physical beauty and high birth and riches, and when their trial takes place they are supported by a crowd of witnesses who come to testify to the righteousness of their lives. c

'This causes confusion to the judges, who are also hampered by being clothed themselves, and their soul is hidden behind eyes and ears and the rest of the body, and all of this, as well as their own clothes and those of the accused form a barrier in front of them. Our first task, then,' said Zeus, 'is to take from mortals the foreknowledge of the hour of their death which they at present enjoy. Prometheus has been given orders[127] to bring this to an end. Next, they must all be tried naked after they have died, and, so that the verdict will be just, the judge too must be naked and dead himself, viewing with bare soul the bare soul of every man as soon as he is d e dead, when he has no friends and relations to aid him and has left behind on earth all his former glory. I realized this before you did, and I have appointed my own sons[128] as judges, two from Asia, Minos and Rhadamanthus, and one from Europe, Aeacus. These, when they are dead, shall sit in judgement in the meadow at the parting of the ways from which the two roads lead, the one to the Isles of the Blessed and the other to Tartarus. Rhadamanthus shall try the men of Asia and Aeacus the men of Europe, but to Minos I will give the supreme function of delivering judgement when his colleagues are in doubt. This will ensure that the judgement about the ultimate destiny of mortals is decided as justly as possible.'

524

b

This, Callicles, is what I have heard and believe to be true, and from this account I draw the following conclusions. Death, it seems to me, is nothing but the complete separation of two separate entities, body and soul, and, when this separation takes place, each of them is left in much the same state as when the person was alive.[129] The body retains its natural characteristics with the consequences of its treatment and experience all still visible. For instance, if a man's body during life has grown large by nature or nurture or both, his corpse will be large in death; if fat, his corpse will be fat, and so on. Again, if the deceased was in the habit of wearing his hair long, his corpse will be long-haired; if he was a convict, whose body was marked during life with the scars of blows inflicted by whips or in other ways, the same marks will be visible on his body after death; if his limbs were broken or deformed in life, you will see the same when he is dead. In a word, all or almost all the physical characteristics which a person has acquired during life remain visible for a time even after death. The same, I believe, Callicles, is true of the soul; once it is stripped of the body all its qualities may be seen, not only its natural endowments but the modifications brought about by the various habits which its owner has formed.

c

d

So when the dead reach the judgement-seat, in the case of Asiatics the judgement seat of Rhadamanthus, Rhadamanthus summons them before him and inspects each

e

person's soul, without knowing to whom it belongs. Often, when it is the king of Persia or some other monarch or potentate that he has to deal with, he finds that there is no soundness in the soul whatever; it is a mass of weals and scars imprinted on it by various acts of perjury and wrongdoing 525 which have been stamped on his soul; it is twisted and warped by lies and vanity and has grown crooked because truth has had no part in its development. Power, luxury, pride and debauchery have left it so full of disproportion and ugliness that when he has inspected it Rhadamanthus dispatches it in ignominy straight to prison, where on its arrival it will undergo the appropriate treatment.

The object of all punishment which is rightly inflicted b should be either to improve and benefit its subjects or else to make them an example to others, who will be deterred by the sight of their sufferings and reform their own conduct. Those who are helped by undergoing punishment, whether by gods or men, are those whose faults are curable; yet both here and in Hades this benefit comes only at the cost of pain and anguish; there is no other way in which men can be cured of wrongdoing. Those who have committed the worst crimes and are consequently incurable become examples to others. c Being incurable they are no longer capable of receiving benefit themselves, but they do good to others, who see them suffering an eternity of the most severe and painful and terrible torment on account of their sins. They are literally hung up as object-lessons there in the prison-house of Hades, in order that every newly arrived wrongdoer may contemplate them and take the warning to heart.[130]

If what Polus says about him is true, I maintain that Arche- d laus[131] will be one of these, together with any other tyrant of like character. Indeed, I think that the majority of these warning examples are drawn from among tyrants and kings and potentates and politicians, whose power gives them the opportunity of committing the greatest and worst impieties. In support of this view I can quote Homer, in whose Hades e those whose punishment is everlasting, Tantalus and Sisyphus and Tityus, are kings and potentates, whereas Thersites – and any other common criminal – has never been represented as suffering the extremity of punishment assigned to the incurable. The reason is, I think, that he did not have sufficient power for wrongdoing, and to that extent was more fortunate than those who did.[132]

526 However, Callicles, even if the extremely wicked are found among men in power, there is nothing to prevent good men arising in this class, and those who do so are greatly to be admired. For it is difficult, Callicles, and very praiseworthy, to live a life rightly when there is ample opportunity to do wrong. But such men are rare. There have been, both here and in other countries, and no doubt there will be in the future, fine, good men who have shone in the righteous conduct of affairs committed to their charge; one of the most illustrious, b Aristides[133] the son of Lysimachus, won a reputation which extended over the whole of Greece; but the majority of men in power, my friend, go to the bad.

As I was saying, then, when Rhadamanthus gets such a person before him, he is quite ignorant of his identity or parentage; his knowledge is confined to the man's guilt, and having considered this and made a mark to indicate whether he regards him as curable or incurable, he dispatches him c to Tartarus, where he undergoes the appropriate treatment. But sometimes the eye of the judge lights on a soul which has lived in purity and truth; it may or may not be the soul of a private person, but most often, Callicles, if I am not mistaken, it is the soul of a lover of wisdom who has kept to his own calling during his life and has not meddled in city affairs.[134] Then Rhadamanthus is struck with admiration and sends him off to the Isles of the Blessed. Aeacus discharges the same judicial function, holding, like Rhadamanthus, a staff of office in his hand; Minos, who sits as president of the court, enjoys the unique distinction of a golden sceptre – you may d remember that Odysseus in Homer says that he saw him 'wielding a sceptre of gold and pronouncing judgement among the dead'.[135]

Personally, Callicles, I put faith in this story, and make it my aim to present my soul to its judge in the soundest possible state. That is why, dismissing from consideration the honours which stimulate most people's ambition, and pursuing the truth, I shall try to be as good as possible, both in life and, when my time comes to die, in death. To this way of life and (e) to this struggle, in which the prize, I assure you, outweighs all the prizes of this world, I challenge all others to the best of my ability. In your case, Callicles, it is a counter-challenge, coupled with a warning that when the time comes for you to stand the trial of which I have just spoken, you will be quite unable to defend yourself; you will stand at the judgement- (527) seat of the son of Aegina, when he summons you before him, as gaping and dizzy as I will be here,[136] and possibly someone will slap you in the face with impunity and subject you to every kind of insult.

Perhaps you may despise what I have told you as no more than an old wives' tale. There would be every reason why you should if our search had disclosed to us any better or truer account of the matter; but as things are you see that the three of you, yourself and Polus and Gorgias, the wisest men in (b) Greece, are unable to show that there is any better way of life than this one now, which also turns out to benefit us in the world to come. All the other theories put forward in our long conversation have been refuted and this conclusion alone stands firm: that one should avoid doing wrong with more care than being wronged, and that the supreme object of a man's efforts, in public and in private life, must be the reality rather than the appearance of goodness. Moreover, if a person goes wrong in any way he must be punished, and the next best thing to being good is to become good by submitting to punishment and paying the penalty for one's faults. Every form of pandering, whether to oneself or to others, whether (c) to large groups or to small, is to be shunned; oratory is to be employed always in the service of right, and the same holds true of every other activity.

Be guided by me then and join me in the pursuit of what, as our argument shows, will secure your happiness both in life and after death. Let people despise you for a fool and insult you if they wish; yes, by Zeus, even if they inflict the ultimate indignity of a blow in the face, take it cheerfully: if d you are really a good man devoted to the practice of virtue they can do you no harm.

And then, when we have adequately exercised ourselves in this way in partnership with one another, finally we can, if we think fit, set our hand to politics or to giving our opinion about any other subject that attracts us: our opinions will be better worth having then than they are now. It would be shameful for men in our present condition, who are so uneducated that we never think the same for two moments together, even on subjects of the greatest importance, to give ourselves the airs of persons of importance. Let us then allow e ourselves to be led by the argument now made clear to us, which teaches that the best way of life is to practise righteousness and all virtue, whether living or dying; let us follow that way and urge others to follow it, instead of the way which you in mistaken confidence are urging upon me, for that way is worthless, Callicles.

This last section raises the question of what is the status of the story, i.e. what does Socrates mean when he asserts that it is 'the truth' (523a2)? The boundaries between muthos *(story, myth) and* logos *(rational account – 'fact') are not as clear-cut as the words might imply to a modern audience; in saying that it is true, a* logos, *Socrates is asserting its moral relevance as much as its literal truth: on other occasions Plato has Socrates express less precise views about the afterlife (e.g.* Apology, *40c ff.). In adapting a traditional picture of judgement after death found in poets such as Homer (eighth century* BC*) and Pindar (fifth century* BC*), Plato is having Socrates validate on a divine and cosmic level the conclusions reached by logical argument in the rest of the dialogue, as he makes explicit in the concluding sections of the work.*

This leads, however, to the more difficult question of the relationship between the story and the rest of the dialogue. In terms of the issues the relationship is clear, for example both the previous sections and the final one discuss the relationship of soul to body, improvement of the soul by punishment, the rarity of good lives among those in power. Yet, if Socrates' arguments in the dialogue taken as a whole are valid and if he has by this point (523a) succeeded in demonstrating that a good life is its own reward, so to speak, why is further validation necessary? Does the presence of the myth imply some basic inadequacy in the argumentation up to this point? Does it constitute some higher or more authoritative statement of the truth which Socrates is attempting to put over – a view which is not entirely consistent with Socrates' quite unaccustomed confidence in his own reasoning expressed in Gorgias *as a whole (see especially 508e ff.)? These are difficult issues to which there is no clear-cut answer.*

One clue, however, might be found in the dramatic structure of the dialogue. In the immediately preceding discussion with Callicles, Socrates has, quite unusually in the Platonic dialogues, totally failed to convince this interlocutor of the truth of what he has said; although ostensibly defeated and paying intermittent lip-service to Socrates, Callicles remains impervious to logical arguments and stubbornly asserts his opposition at intervals, forcing an unaccustomed continuous and dogmatic form of discourse from Socrates (the makrologia *for which he apologizes earlier). This may be linked to early stages in Plato's growing awareness of the limitations of the* elenchus*; logic does not suffice for Socrates to persuade those who will not be persuaded (see e.g. Beversluis 2000, pp. 356 ff.). So Plato may have Socrates resort to the myth as a mode of persuasion perhaps more likely to have some effect on his stubborn interlocutor. However, if this is the case, Plato does not ostensibly present Socrates' tactic as succeeding; Socrates concludes the dialogue without any sign of assent from Callicles. (On this, see the Introduction, 'Socrates and the "good life"'.)*

The Gorgias *myth may also be seen in a broader context as the first (and in many ways the least developed) of a series of Platonic myths of the fate of the individual after death which conclude the later dialogues,* Phaedo *and* Republic. *While drawing heavily on traditional and popular beliefs concerning the fate of the soul after death, in these myths Plato can be seen to tailor the stories to, and even invent details to harmonize with, the thrust of the main argument of the dialogue (see especially Annas 1982). Hence the silence in* Gorgias *on the ultimate fate of the souls of the dead (a key theme in the* Republic *myth) in favour of an emphasis on the appropriateness and inevitability of their punishment.*

Notes

1. *late for a feast*: The proverb was apparently something like 'first at a feast, last at a battle'.
2. *What do you mean?*: Requests to Socrates for further clarification occur frequently, and often indicate the introduction of an idea which may not be immediately clear to Plato's external audience as well as those in the dialogue.
3. *His brother*: Polygnotus, a notable painter of the fifth century BC, famous for his decoration of the Stoa Poikile at Athens, here strangely – from our point of view – anonymous.
4. *There are . . . all*: This speech is in a mannered, sophistic style, with verbal repetition and antithesis, e.g. *empeiria/apeiria* = 'experience/lack of experience', *techne/tuche* = 'art/chance'; probably a Platonic parody, but possibly from an existing work of Polus. See 462b11 for Socrates' mention of having read Polus' treatise.
5. '*I boast myself to be*': A Homeric formulaic phrase, e.g. *Iliad* 6.211.
6. *By Hera*: Not normally an exclamation used by men, but apparently habitually used by Socrates (found in Xenophon as well as Plato) and always accompanying approving (if, on occasion, as here, ironical) comments.
7. *good at: Dunatos* = 'capable of', 'powerful at', i.e. what constitutes mastery of an 'art'.
8. *good too . . . speak*: Socrates plays on the ambiguity of *logos* = both 'speech, words' and '*rational* account'; Gorgias naturally understands the former, but Socrates gradually makes it clear that the latter is what he has in mind.
9. *physical training*: One of the three staples of basic education at Athens (the others being training in literacy and music).
10. *arithmetic . . . calculation*: The distinction is between the theory of number and the practical skill of reckoning.

11. *backgammon*: Olympiodorus (sixth-century AD commentator on *Gorgias*) suggests that the speech element in this game consisted in 'calling the throws' (see Dodds 1959, p. 197).
12. *may stand*: A stock official formula, to avoid needless repetition.
13. *well-known song . . . come by*: This *skolion* (traditional drinking song performed at the *symposium* (wine-party)) is quoted by later authors as follows: 'For a mortal man health is best; second to be born naturally handsome; third to be rich without deceit; and fourth to be in the flower of youth with one's friends' (Plato omits the fourth member, as not being relevant to his point here).
14. *jury . . . may be*: All these gatherings involve, in Athens, large groups of people.
15. *conviction: Peitho* = both the process of persuasion and the result ('conviction') and was a key concept in the writings of the historical Gorgias.
16. *Zeuxis*: Greek painter of the late fifth century BC, famous for his lifelike renderings; his paintings of grapes were said to have deceived birds.
17. *right and wrong*: Literally 'what is just and what is unjust'; the Greek adjective *dikaios* can be narrowly so translated to distinguish it from terms referring to the other traditional virtues, e.g. temperance, bravery etc., but the polarity *dikaios/adikos* frequently has a broader ethical range in Greek, which corresponds to 'right/wrong'. See Glossary of Greek Terms.
18. *mass of people . . . time*: Socrates believed that serious teaching had to be one to one (or in very small groups).
19. *appoint medical officers*: At Athens state physicians were appointed by the Assembly and paid for out of public funds. Other 'professional workers' (*demiourgoi*) would be appointed as specialists from time to time.
20. *Themistocles*: In 479 BC, immediately after the Persian Wars, the Athenians refortified Athens and the port of the Piraeus on the initiative of the statesman Themistocles.
21. *Middle Wall*: The 'Long Walls' were built in the early 450s BC as a fortification linking Athens with the coastal ports of Phaleron and Piraeus. The 'Middle Wall' was built on the advice of Pericles in the 440s close to the northern wall and, like it, joining Athens and Piraeus (and the original southern wall was abandoned). All these developments were designed to enhance Athens as a sea power.
22. *spite: Phthonos* = 'jealousy (at the success of another)'; the negative aspect of the competitive ethos of Greek society.

23. *disgrace: Aischron* = 'shameful', a strong value-term (here with negative connotation) implying that Gorgias is worried about public loss of face: see also B[5] below.
24. *do you remember ... ago*: 456d ff., A[4].
25. *By the dog*: An allusion to the dog-headed god Anubis (see 482b5). A favourite colloquialism of Socrates, also found in Old Comedy.
26. *who do you imagine*: Picks up 'Or do you imagine ...' in b4, with the grammar changed by the intervening sentences. Plato makes Polus' confused utterance reflect the pent-up emotion of his outburst (see his earlier barging into the conversation at 448a6).
27. *at the beginning ... conversation*: At 448c4 above.
28. *treatise I read lately*: Likely to be called 'The Art of Rhetoric' or some such. Nothing further is known about this.
29. *experience: Empeiria* – the word (over)used by Polus in his abortive speech at 448c4 ff., without, of course, the pejorative implication Socrates gives it here.
30. The distribution of words between Socrates and Polus in these last two lines is uncertain; the above distribution, which goes back to Olympiodorus (and adopted by Dodds 1959, p. 224), accentuates the humour of characterization: when Polus tries to take over the questioning, Socrates has to feed him his lines! This passage amounts to a parody of the standard Socratic *elenchus*, the investigation of a topic by question and answer.
31. *argument ... subject*: Tact, liberally laced with irony – the discussion at A[3–4] above shed plenty of light on Gorgias' views!
32. *pandering: Kolakeia* = 'flattery', an activity which 'panders to public taste instead of trying to educate it' (Dodds 1959, p. 225).
33. *where oratory stands ... ask away*: Socrates is feeding Polus his lines again! See n. 30 above.
34. *Polus ... youth*: There is probably a pun intended on Polus' name here: *polos* = 'colt'.
35. *soul ... body*: The division of the individual into body (*soma*) and soul (*psyche*), taken over from Greek popular belief, assumes major importance for Plato's ethics later in this dialogue and elsewhere.
36. *cookery ... hunger*: The imitating of real by spurious arts here is presented in terms of images from Athenian theatrical performance (where actors wore masks), e.g. 'puts on the mask', 'compete before an audience'.
37. *geometrical proportion ... justice*: See the diagram at the beginning of this section, B[1].

38. *sophists . . . orators*; Sophists were teachers of moral and political affairs, orators were practitioners (but both were on the wrong side of Plato's line between genuine and spurious arts).
39. *Anaxagoras . . . mixed up*: A natural scientist from Clazomenae in Asia Minor who came to Athens in the 450s BC. The words quoted by Socrates here out of context come from the beginning of Anaxagoras' treatise, in which he envisaged a primal mixture of all things in the universe before the intervention of Mind began the process of discrimination.
40. *thought of*: A play here on *nomizesthai* = 'to be thought of' or 'to be esteemed, to count'.
41. *tyrants*: The epitome of absolute rulers, in the fifth and fourth centuries still quite common in cities in, for example, Italy and Sicily, but proverbial in democratic Athens for arbitrary, oppressive and violent behaviour. The assumed link with orators (albeit somewhat exaggerated by Plato for purposes of the argument) underlines the political power skilled public speakers had in a society still largely dependent on the spoken word (see the Introduction, 'The cultural background').
42. *By the –*: Socrates stops himself in the midst of one of his favourite oaths ('By the dog!').
43. *alliterative style*: 'Peerless Polus' translates '*o loiste Pole*', the effect of the exact vowel repetition not being possible in English, it has been effectively turned (by Hamilton) into a consonantal (alliterative) jingle.
44. *Archelaus . . . Macedonia*: Archelaus succeeded his father as absolute monarch in Macedonia *c.* 413 BC, and reigned until his assassination in 399. He was on friendly terms with Athens and invited artists and writers, including the famous tragedian Euripides, who died at his court.
45. *Great King*: The conventional Greek way of referring to the king of Persia.
46. *honourable and good: Kalon kai agathon* (See Glossary of Greek Terms); the traditional appellation of an Athenian 'gentleman', but given new ethical content by Socrates, and note Socrates' inclusion of the female sex here, not usually part of the predominantly male value-system.
47. *Of course . . . Archelaus*: The whole of Polus' speech here is heavily sarcastic; he does not, of course, actually believe that Archelaus is miserable!
48. *Nicias . . . Dionysus*: Nicias, the Athenian conservative politician and one of the leaders of the Athenian expedition to Sicily, died

there in 413 BC (see Thucydides, *History of the Peloponnesian War*, Books 6 and 7). The tripods were prizes won by him and his family as *choregi*, successful providers of the Chorus at Athenian dramatic festivals; the precinct of Dionysus, where the tripods were offered, is appropriately sited next to the theatre of that name, where the well-known tragedies and comedies were performed.

49. *Aristocrates*: A member of the oligarchic faction of the 400, which briefly came to power in Athens in 411 BC.
50. *Pericles*: The most famous Athenian statesman of the fifth century (*c.* 495–429 BC).
51. *law courts ... truth*: The image of a law-court dispute over property – in this case the truth – is maintained here.
52. *I said earlier ... wrong*: At 469b9.
53. *frighten ... bogeys*: Literally, 'frighten me with Mormo'. Mormo was a bogey-woman invoked to frighten children.
54. *chosen by lot ... correct procedure*: Under the Athenian democratic constitution, a Council (*Boule*) of 500 was chosen by lot for one year, and fifty citizens from each of the ten Athenian tribes in turn formed a standing committee; during this period one of the committee was chosen as president (*epistates*) of the Assembly. Socrates' reference appears to be to a celebrated occasion in 406 BC when his tribe (Alopeke) formed the committee, and as president on the day he refused to allow an illegal mass trial of generals after the sea battle of Arginusae; if this is the occasion to which Socrates is referring (and we know of no other), 'provoked laughter by my ignorance of the correct procedure' seems an inappropriately light-hearted way to refer to a grave crisis in the later stages of the Peloponnesian War, with personal danger for Socrates himself; contrast the tone with which he refers to the incident in *Apology* 32a–b.
55. *good*: Polus' substitution of 'good' (*agathos*) for 'useful' (*ophelimos*) here appears to be presented as an unconscious concession which paves the way for Socrates' proof.
56. *just: Dikaios* is here given its more precise translation of 'just' in this section (given the context of wrongdoing and punishment); for the range of meaning of *dikaios*, see Glossary of Greek Terms.
57. *To sum up ... does*: As Aristotle noted (*Rhetoric* 1397a30), not all correlatives work as well as Socrates' examples here suggest; 'If I inflict pain with difficulty, it does not follow that you suffer pain with difficulty ...' (Irwin 1979, p. 159), and see next note.

58. *Then the man . . . him*: This does not logically follow (see previous note). 'If the punishing of B is a good action, B's being punished must also be good . . . [but] from this it is illegitimately inferred that being punished is good *for* B' (Dodds 1959, p. 252).
59. *O Callicles*: Formal address. See 482c below where Callicles addresses Socrates, possibly with ironical undertones.
60. *Alcibiades*: A notable, not to say notorious, Athenian statesman who died in 404 BC; for his erotic relationship with Socrates, as presented by Plato, see *Symposium* 212d5 ff.
61. *Demos . . . Pyrilampes*: Pyrilampes was Plato's stepfather; Demos was a wealthy and handsome man mentioned by Aristophanes (*Wasps* 98, produced in 422). There is difficulty in making the supposed dramatic date (see the Introduction, 'Socrates and Plato') fit all the individuals and relationships, and one suspects that Plato has introduced the Callicles–Demos relationship at least, for the sake of the pun on *demos*.
62. *mass of mankind . . . myself*: For this idea see B[4] above.
63. *foundation in . . . nature*: The polarity 'nature' and 'convention (law)' (*physis* and *nomos*) was influential in fifth-century debates over the origins and status of society and its laws (in sophists such as Antiphon and the historian Thucydides). See further Waterfield 2000, pp. 258 ff.
64. *take two . . . countless instances*: The reference is to the invasions of the Persian kings Xerxes and his father Darius in 480 and 510 BC respectively, the failure of both providing, it would seem, a less than convincing example for Callicles to cite!
65. *'Law . . . price' . . . superior*: The context of this Pindaric fragment is unknown, and it is unlikely that the original poem would have borne Callicles' interpretation of it. Geryon was a giant with three bodies and three heads, and the theft of his cattle was one of Heracles' most celebrated exploits.
66. *Every man . . . days*: From Euripides' fragmentary play *Antiope*, which features a verbal exchange between the sons of Antiope – Zethus a herdsman and Amphion a musician – on the competing merits of the practical and contemplative life. Their opposing claims, and their relevance to the 'two lives' represented by Callicles and Socrates, are an ongoing theme in *Gorgias*.
67. *slavish ring about it*: Slaves were considered precocious, and so able to talk clearly, through being set to work very young.
68. *'men win renown'*: The poet is Homer (*Iliad* 9.441).
69. *if . . . death penalty*: See n. 136.

70. *'abandon argument . . . house'*: Further quotations from Euripides' *Antiope* (see n. 66 above).
71. *Tisander . . . Cholargeis*: Wealthy associates of Callicles, generally politically right wing, and on the fringes of the intellectual world of the sophists.
72. *ashamed . . . verbal traps*: Callicles is being disingenuous here; Socrates is merely exposing lack of clarity which lies at the basis of the definition.
73. *ironic Socrates*: 'Ironic' here implies that Callicles believes (rightly!) that Socrates is ridiculing him by reversing the actual relationship – Socrates has been playing the schoolmaster (on Socratic 'irony' in this passage, see Vlastos 1991, pp. 25–6). Socrates responds in the following line by recalling Callicles' mockery of him (see 484e ff. above).
74. *clarifying nothing*: Socrates' point here is that Callicles, in being forced to define 'better' (*beltious*) in e5, instead simply offers a verbal equivalent, a synonym (*ameinous*), which is translated here as 'nobler'.
75. *But what . . . there?*: Translating Burnet's text here. Dodds 1959 breaks the line up, giving Callicles an extra exclamation in the middle: 'what's that?' It is certainly plausible that Socrates' cryptic utterance here demands further clarification!
76. *As I said before*: At 483b ff.
77. *virtue and happiness: Arete* and *eudaimonia*. Callicles' highly paradoxical redefinition of these key positive value-terms represents them as, he claims, they 'naturally' are.
78. *Who knows if . . . life?*: From Euripides, either *Phrixus* or *Polyidos*, a characteristically startling paradox made fun of by Aristophanes in *Frogs* 1082 and 1477 ff.
79. *Our body . . . buried*: The punning idea that the body (*soma*) was the tomb (*sema*) in which the soul (*psyche*) is buried was a popular religious idea (also found in Pythagorean philosophy) which had much influence on Plato.
80. *Sicilian . . . Italian*: 'Sicilian' probably refers to the fifth-century BC philosopher Empedocles; 'Italian' suggests the Pythagoreans.
81. *he labels fools . . . up*: The plays on words here are untranslatable: the part of the soul containing the appetites is called a 'pitcher' (*pithos*) because it is easily influenced (*pithanos*). The 'fools' (*anoetous*) are 'uninitiated' (*amyetous*). Puns like this were taken seriously by Greeks (and not just Plato) as indicating significant connections between words of similar sound.

82. *Hades . . . invisible world*: 'Hades' was supposed to derive in a folk etymology from the Greek *aides* = 'invisible'.
83. *uninitiated . . . leaky sieve*: This recalls the fate of the daughters of Danaus, whose punishment in the myth was to pour water eternally into leaky vessels. Plato's allegorization of mythical and religious material here is characteristic.
84. *greedy and messy bird*: This may be a stone-curlew, which lives near streams or torrents (*charadrai*) – hence the name; it was said by an ancient commentator to excrete while it eats, hence the appropriateness of the allusion here.
85. *Archarnae . . . Alopece*: Each speaker addresses the other with a mock formality which includes their *demes* (districts of Athens from which they come).
86. *It is not . . . Callicles*: The translation is not certain here; the phrase *ou sé hauté hé timé* could also mean: 'It is not for you to estimate their [i.e. the questions'] value, Callicles' (Dodds 1959, p. 313; but surely that is just what Callicles ought to be doing!).
87. *happy man . . . allowed*: The Eleusinian Mysteries consisted of preliminary rites (the Lesser Mysteries), initiation into which had to precede initiation proper (the Greater Mysteries). Socrates sarcastically commends Callicles for being happy in his ability to dispense with the preliminary steps of the argument.
88. *If you remember . . . good*: At 467c5 ff. above. Socrates' (or Plato's) memory is not accurate here: what they actually agreed earlier was that all actions were *as a matter of fact* performed as a means to the good.
89. *god of friendship*: Callicles has on several occasions professed himself well-disposed towards Socrates (e.g. 485e2).
90. *choruses . . . poetry*: The dithyramb was a choral song in honour of the god Dionysus, and performed, along with tragedy, at the festival of the Great Dionysia at Athens.
91. *Cinesias*: A poet who composed dithyrambs, active in the last twenty years of the fifth century and ridiculed by Aristophanes in *Birds* and elsewhere.
92. *Meles*: Described in a fragment of the comic poet Pherecrates (*c.* 420 BC) as the worst singer to the lyre in the world.
93. *Cimon . . . Militiades . . . Pericles*: On these three statesmen, see B[10] below. Pericles died in 429, when Socrates would have been about forty years old.
94. *I don't know . . . carefully*: Translating Dodds's text here; Burnet regards Callicles' reply as part of the end of Socrates' speech (and there are further textual complications); he gives the beginning of

Socrates' following speech (d5) to Callicles as, possibly a sarcastic retort, presumably to be translated 'You will find someone if you look carefully' – referring to the 'men' at the end of Socrates' previous speech.

95. *Epicharmus*: A Sicilian writer of comedy, active during the early fifth century.
96. *others agree with me*: Possibly also including the bystanders, mentioned at 458c.
97. *Amphion . . . Zethus*: See 484e5 ff. and n. 66 above. By 'a speech of Amphion' Socrates means that given time he would assert, against the Zethus of Euripides' play, the value of his own way of life – which he actually does in the last sections of the dialogue.
98. *perfectly good . . . does well*: Plato plays on the ambiguity of *eu prattein* = 'to fare well' i.e. be happy and flourish, and 'to act well', i.e. do what is morally right. Of course, even if he recognized the ambiguity, he would have regarded these as identical ends.
99. *doctrine of unfair shares*: Socrates is talking about 'proportional equality', or shares based on merit; he is carefully placing himself between Callicles' 'excess' and democratic equality, i.e. equal shares for all.
100. *What follows . . . employed*: Socrates is referring here to Callicles' intervention in the dialogue with Polus at 481b5 ff. above.
101. *Polus . . . not to admit*: At 461b above.
102. '*birds of a feather*': Found in Homer, *Odyssey* 17.218: 'as the god always brings like to like'.
103. *two drachmae*: A drachma was, at the end of the fifth century, the standard wage per day for a labourer, and there were six obols in a drachma. Plato's charges here seem very low (possibly to emphasize Socrates' point?).
104. *despise him . . . yourself*: Compare the general Athenian aristocratic contempt for 'mechanical' professions.
105. *the women . . . destiny*: This probably refers to fatalistic sayings common among Athenian women (rather than any literary reference); see Dodds 1959, pp. 349–50.
106. *draw the moon . . . sky*: I.e. causing an eclipse of the moon, a typical feat ascribed to Thessalian witches (Thessaly was an area in Northern Greece). There was also a widespread belief that witchcraft rewarded those who practised it or their families with blindness or paralysis, hence the proverb: 'you are bringing down the moon on yourself'.
107. *Pyrilampes*: See n. 61.
108. *at an earlier stage*: At 500b.

109. *apprenticeship . . . wine-jar*: Proverbial in Greek for attempting complex activities without first mastering the basic skills.
110. *payment . . . ears*: Young oligarchs who adopted Spartan dress and traditional activities, e.g. boxing (hence 'cauliflower ears'). For Plato's presentation of payment for civic activities, see editorial comment at the end of C[10].
111. *Pericles . . . evil*: In 430 BC (related in Thucydides 2.59 ff.). See editorial comment at end of C[10].
112. *the virtuous are gentle*: Possibly an inference from e.g. Homer, *Odyssey* 6.120 ('fierce and not just', so, by implication the just are gentle); or, more plausibly, from a lost epic under Homer's name.
113. *Cimon . . . ostracize . . . ten years*: Ostracism was a form of temporary exile (ten years), without loss of rights or property, for unpopular politicians, who were voted out, their names being inscribed on potsherds (*ostraka*). Cimon had continued the war against the Persians following their invasion and won a victory at the river Eurymedon (Asia Minor) in 468 BC. An oligarch in politics, he was ostracized in 461 for his friendship with Sparta, but subsequently recalled to make a truce with them in 457; he died in 450 fighting against the Persians in Cyprus.
114. *Themistocles . . . exile*: The general responsible for the Athenian naval victory over the Persians at Salamis in 480 BC was ostracized *c.* 472 for reasons which are obscure. Later he was condemned for treason and fled to the Persian court, and was rewarded with the governorship of Magnesia (south-west Asia Minor), where he died.
115. *Miltiades . . . him*: Miltiades, father of Cimon (see 516d5 ff. and n. 113), had famously defeated the Persians at the battle of Marathon (490 BC) but was subsequently condemned for using Athenian forces in a private venture – an abortive attack on the island of Paros. He was heavily fined and escaped death, according to Herodotus, *History* 6.136, because of his former services. The 'pit' was the place where executed criminals were thrown.
116. *provide the city . . . like*: The period in which the dialogue is set, the late fifth century, obviously makes the reference to the 'achievements' of Themistocles and Pericles, but Plato, composing in the early fourth century, may also have had in mind the rebuilding of the Long Walls and the Athenian navy in the 390s BC, of which he obviously disapproved (see especially 519a–b below).
117. *Thearion . . . Sarambus*: Thearion was a well-known Athenian

baker, mentioned in Old Comedy; Mithaecus was a pre-eminent cookery writer from Syracuse – a place known for its culinary luxury; Sarambus is unknown outside this reference.

118. *they will . . . attack you*: Dodds 1959, p. 13, suggests that this might be a hint of the fate of a historical Callicles (see the Introduction, 'The characters of *Gorgias*', and n. 19 there).

119. *nothing to choose . . . former*: For the distinction between sophists and orators see 465c above and n. 38. The sophistic profession was despised by gentleman politicians like Callicles (see also Anytus in *Meno* 91c ff.) as being socially unacceptable and morally subversive; orators, mainly foreigners (such as Gorgias) were seen as providing a useful service in training aspiring politicians in the practice of public speaking. For Socrates, both professions were tarred with the same brush.

120. *if you prefer . . . offensive*: Literally, 'if you prefer to call it Mysian'. The people of Mysia (north-west Asia Minor) were proverbially regarded as the lowest of the low.

121. '*niceties*': Callicles had criticized Socrates in these terms in a quotation from Euripides' *Antiope* at 486c to denigrate his activity; Socrates now throws the accusation back at him as a description of forensic quibbles designed to propitiate a jury.

122. *I shall be judged . . . loudly*: Plato here constructs a detailed comic parody of his presentation of the real trial of Socrates: the jury are children; moral corruption (in the real charge) becomes ruin, allegedly caused by harmful medical treatment; the 'uproar' from the jury recalls the *thorubos* ('din') which punctuated Socrates' defence (see e.g. *Apology* 20e). There is, of course, a serious point to all this: Socrates sees himself as the doctor whose medicine is unacceptable to the Athenian people, who react like children.

123. *We must think so*: Burnet attributes these words to Callicles; but Dodds's attribution of them to Socrates (p. 371) as a firm correction of Callicles' grudging response seems to make more sense of the interchange.

124. *Legendary . . . truth*: 'Legendary tale' translates *muthos*; 'fact' translates *logos*, which has a basic meaning of 'word' or 'story', but also implies a '*rational* account'; for a discussion of how far, and in what sense the story of the afterlife is 'the truth' for Plato, see the editorial comment at the end of C[12].

125. *divided . . . between them*: In Homer (*Iliad* 15.187 ff.), Zeus takes the Heavens, Poseidon the sea and Pluto the Underworld. Socrates presents a bowdlerized version of the succession story; 'succeeded' replaces the violent overthrow of Kronos related in Hesiod's

Theogony 453 ff. Plato elsewhere objects to this story on moral grounds, e.g. *Republic* 377e ff.

126. *I will put . . . happens*: The short sentences of Zeus' pronouncements reflect the simple narrative style of the Greek at this point.
127. *take . . . foreknowledge . . . orders*: Prometheus ('Foresight') can also take away foreknowledge; possibly here there is an echo of Aeschylus, *Prometheus Bound* 248 ff., where Prometheus explains that he stopped mortals from foreseeing their fate by giving them 'blind hopefulness', or the story may go back to an ancient folk-tale source.
128. *my own sons*: All three were traditionally judges in Hades. Minos and Rhadamanthus were from Crete (which was reckoned as part of Asia) and Aeacus was born on the island named after his mother Aegina (near Athens).
129. *Death . . . alive*: For the doctrine, see 493a2–3 above and n. 79.
130. *object-lessons . . . heart*: This only makes sense if the curable souls return again to the upper world. This is the theory of the transmigration of souls, which Plato expounds in detail later in *Republic*, but which does not feature explicitly in *Gorgias*, although the doctrine here seems to presuppose it.
131. *Archelaus*: See B[3] above and n. 44.
132. *Homer . . . who did*: For the punishment of Tantalus, Sisyphus and Tityus, see *Odyssey* 11.576–600. Thersites was a subordinate in the Greek army at Troy who abused the leaders of the expedition and got punished by Odysseus for his insubordination (*Iliad* 2.211 ff.).
133. *Aristides*: Known as 'the Just', he took a prominent part in the battles of the Persian Wars and the political aftermath. Since he was ostracized (483 BC) and so on Socrates' earlier criteria (see C[10] above) must have failed to improve the Athenian people since they turned against him, Plato is being somewhat inconsistent in differentiating him from other statesmen like Pericles.
134. *not meddled . . . affairs*: Socrates here recommends the *apragmosune* ('detachment from political affairs') of the private citizen over *polupragmosune* ('involvement in political affairs') – an important tension in fifth-century politics. See the Amphion and Zethus debate in Euripides' *Antiope*, above n. 66.
135. *Minos . . . 'wielding . . . dead'*: Homer, *Odyssey* 11.569.
136. *gaping and dizzy . . . here*: Not Socrates' demeanour at his actual trial, according to Plato's *Apology*! But note that there is a non-Platonic tradition that Socrates offered no defence at his trial.

Glossary of Greek Terms

Value-terms

adikia (ἀδικία): 'injustice', 'wrongdoing', 'wickedness'; noun corresponding to *adikos*.
adikos (ἄδικος): 'unjust', 'wrong'.
agathos (ἀγαθός): 'good', with comparative adjectives: *beltion*, *kreitton*, *ameinon*, (βελτίων, κρείττων, ἀμείνων) = 'better', 'stronger'.
aischros (αἴσχρος): 'shameful', 'ugly', 'base', opposite of *kalos* (see below); together these are the most powerful terms of general approval/disapproval (see the argument with Polus at 474c ff.).
aischune (αἰσχύνη): 'shame', 'dishonour'; noun corresponding to *aischros*.
akolasia (ἀκολασία): 'intemperance', 'licence', 'lack of moderation', 'lack of discipline'; opposite of *sophrosune*.
arete (ἀρετή): 'excellence', 'virtue', 'well-being'. The general virtue at which Socrates and his fellow conversationalists claim to be aiming, although they all define it differently.
dikaios (δίκαιος): 'just', 'right', opposite of *adikos* (see above).
dike/dikaiosune (δίκη/δικαιοσύνη): 'justice', 'right', 'righteousness', 'uprightness'; the noun corresponding to *dikaios*.
eudaimon (εὐδαίμων): 'happy', 'fortunate', 'prosperous' (*literally*, 'having a good *daimon*, or destiny'). On the ethical problem of the *adikos eudaimon* ('the unjust man who prospers'), see introductory commentary on B[3].
eudaimonia (εὐδαιμονία): 'happiness', 'prosperity'; the noun corresponding to *eudaimon*.
kakia (κακία): 'evil', 'vice'; the noun corresponding to *kakos*.
kakos (κακός): 'bad', 'evil', 'criminal', 'harmful', opposite of *agathos* (see above), with comparative: *kakion* (κακίων) = 'worse', 'more evil', 'more harmful'.
kalos (καλός): 'fine', 'fair', 'beautiful', 'noble', 'honourable'.

kosmios (κόσμιος): 'well-ordered', 'moderate'.
ophelimos (ὠφέλιμος): 'useful', 'beneficial'; often a near synonym for *agathos* (see above).
sophrosune (σωφροσύνη): 'temperance', 'moderation', 'discipline'.

Other terms

doxa (δόξα): 'belief, 'opinion'; as opposed to.
episteme (ἐπιστήμη): 'knowledge'.
nomos (νόμος): 'law', 'convention'.
peitho: (πείθω): 'persuasion'; along with *doxa*, the term with which Socrates and Gorgias define oratory in *Gorgias* (see especially 455a).
physis (φύσις): 'nature', as opposed to *nomos* (see above).
techne (τέχνη): 'art', 'skill', 'craft'; an activity characterized by *episteme* as opposed to *doxa* (see above).

Index

READ MORE IN PENGUIN

In every corner of the world, on every subject under the sun, Penguin represents quality and variety – the very best in publishing today.

For complete information about books available from Penguin – including Puffins and Penguin Classics – and how to order them, write to us at the appropriate address below. Please note that for copyright reasons the selection of books varies from country to country.

In the United Kingdom: *Please write to* Dept EP, Penguin Books Ltd, Bath Road, Harmondsworth, West Drayton, Middlesex UB7 ODA

In the United States: *Please write to* Consumer Services, Penguin Putnam Inc., 405 Murray Hill Parkway, East Rutherford, New Jersey 07073-2136. *VISA and MasterCard holders call 1-800-631-8571 to order Penguin titles*

In Canada: *Please write to* Penguin Books Canada Ltd, 10 Alcorn Avenue, Suite 300, Toronto, Ontario M4V 3B2

In Australia: *Please write to* Penguin Books Australia Ltd, 487 Maroondah Highway, Ringwood, Victoria 3134

In New Zealand: *Please write to* Penguin Books (NZ) Ltd, Private Bag 102902, North Shore Mail Centre, Auckland 10

In India: *Please write to* Penguin Books India Pvt Ltd, 11, Community Centre, Panchsheel Park, New Delhi 110017

In the Netherlands: *Please write to* Penguin Books Netherlands bv, Postbus 3507, NL-1001 AH Amsterdam

In Germany: *Please write to* Penguin Books Deutschland GmbH, Metzlerstrasse 26, 60594 Frankfurt am Main

In Spain: *Please write to* Penguin Books S. A., Bravo Murillo 19, 1°B, 28015 Madrid

In Italy: *Please write to* Penguin Italia s.r.l., Via Vittoria Emanuele 451a, 20094 Corsico, Milano

In France: *Please write to* Penguin France, 12, Rue Prosper Ferradou, 31700 Blagnac

In Japan: *Please write to* Penguin Books Japan Ltd, Iidabashi KM-Bldg, 2-23-9 Koraku, Bunkyo-Ku, Tokyo 112-0004

In South Africa: *Please write to* Penguin Books South Africa (Pty) Ltd, P.O. Box 751093, Gardenview, 2047 Johannesburg

EURIPIDES

Heracles and Other Plays

The dramas Euripides wrote towards the end of his life are remarkable for their stylistic innovation and their adventurous – even outrageous – plots.

Of these plays, *Heracles* stands apart in its stark portrayal of undeserved human suffering and the malignant power of the gods. In contrast the *Cyclops* (Euripides' sole surviving satyr play) celebrates drink, sex and self-indulgent hedonism. While in *Iphigenia among the Taurians*, *Ion* and *Helen*, Euripides exploits the comic potential to be found in traditional myth, weaving plots full of startling shifts of tone, deception and illusion. Alongside the comedy, however, Euripides always reminds us how quickly fortunes are reversed and invites us to view the world with scepticism and compassion.

'One of the best translations of Euripides I have seen' ROBERT FAGLES on John Davie's translation of *Medea and Other Plays*, also in Penguin Classics

'John Davie's translations are outstanding . . . the tone throughout is refreshingly modern yet dignified' WILLIAM ALLAN, *Classical Review*

Translated by JOHN DAVIE
With an introduction by RICHARD RUTHERFORD

EURIPIDES

Medea and Other Plays

'That proud, impassioned soul, so ungovernable now that she has felt the sting of injustice'

Medea, in which a spurned woman takes revenge upon her lover by killing her children, is one of the most shocking of all the Greek tragedies. Dominating the play is Medea herself, a towering figure who demonstrates Euripides' unusual willingness to give voice to a woman's case. *Alcestis*, a tragicomedy, is based on a magical myth in which Death is overcome, and *The Children of Heracles* examines conflict between might and right, while *Hippolytus* deals with self-destructive integrity and moral dilemmas. These plays show Euripides transforming awesome figures of Greek myths into recognizable, fallible human beings.

John Davie's accessible prose translation is accompanied by a general introduction and individual prefaces to each play.

'One of the best prose translations of Euripides I have seen' ROBERT FAGLES

'John Davie's translations are outstanding . . . the tone throughout is refreshingly modern yet dignified' WILLIAM ALLAN, ***Classical Review***

Translated by JOHN DAVIE
With introductions and notes by RICHARD RUTHERFORD

ARISTOPHANES

Lysistrata and Other Plays

'We women have the salvation of Greece in our hands'

Writing at a time of political and social crisis in Athens, Aristophanes (*c.* 447–*c.* 385 BC) was an eloquent, yet bawdy, challenger to the demagogue and the sophist. In *Lysistrata* and *The Acharnians*, two pleas for an end to the long war between Athens and Sparta, a band of women and a lone peasant respectively defeat the political establishment. The darker comedy of *The Clouds* satirizes Athenian philosophers, Socrates in particular, and reflects the uncertainties of a generation in which all traditional religious and ethical beliefs were being challenged.

For this edition Alan Sommerstein has completely revised his translation of the three plays, bringing out the full nuances of Aristophanes' ribald humour and intricate word play, with a new introduction explaining the historical and cultural background to the plays.

Translated with an introduction and notes by
ALAN H. SOMMERSTEIN

PLATO

The Last Days of Socrates

'Nothing can harm a good man either in life or after death'

The trial and condemnation of Socrates on charges of heresy and corrupting young minds is a defining moment in the history of classical Athens. In tracing these events through four dialogues, Plato also developed his own philosophy, based on Socrates' manifesto for a life guided by self-responsibility. *Euthyphro* finds Socrates outside the court-house, debating the nature of piety, while *The Apology* is his robust rebuttal of the charges of impiety and a defence of the philosopher's life. In the *Crito*, while awaiting execution in prison, Socrates counters the arguments of friends urging him to escape. Finally, in the *Phaedo*, he is shown calmly confident in the face of death, skilfully arguing the case for the immortality of the soul.

Hugh Tredennick's landmark 1954 translation has been revised by Harold Tarrant, reflecting changes in Platonic studies, with an introduction and expanded introductions to each of the four dialogues.

Translated by HUGH TREDENNICK *and* HAROLD TARRANT
With an introduction and notes by HAROLD TARRANT

PLATO

The Republic

'We are concerned with the most important of issues, the choice between a good and an evil life'

Plato's *Republic* is widely acknowledged as the cornerstone of Western philosophy. Presented in the form of a dialogue between Socrates and three different interlocutors, it is an inquiry into the notion of a perfect community and the ideal individual within it. During the conversation other questions are raised: what is goodness; what is reality; what is knowledge? *The Republic* also addresses the purpose of education and the roles of both women and men as 'guardians' of the people. With remarkable lucidity and deft use of allegory, Plato arrives at a depiction of a state bound by harmony and ruled by 'philosopher kings'.

Desmond Lee's translation of *The Republic* has come to be regarded as a classic in its own right. His introduction discusses contextual themes such as Plato's disillusionment with Athenian politics and the trial of Socrates. This new edition also features a revised bibliography.

Translated with an introduction by DESMOND LEE